The Red River in Southwestern History

THE
RED RIVER
IN SOUTHWESTERN
HISTORY

By Carl Newton Tyson

UNIVERSITY OF OKLAHOMA PRESS : NORMAN

078305

By Carl Newton Tyson

The Pawnee People (Phoenix, 1977)
The McMan: The Lives of Robert M. McFarlin and James A. Chapman
   (with James Thomas and Odie Faulk) (Norman, 1977)
The Gentleman: The Life of Joseph LaFortune (with Odie Faulk and
   James Thomas) (Oklahoma City, 1979)
The Red River in Southwestern History (Norman, 1981)

Library of Congress Cataloging in Publication Data

Tyson, Carl N.
   The Red River in southwestern history.

   Bibliography: p.
   Includes index.
   1. Red River Valley (Tex.-La.)—History.   2. Red River (Tex.-
La.)—History.   I. Title.
F377.R3T95   976.6′6   81-40292
                     AACR2

F
377
.R3
T95
1981

For
Toni, Jon, Matthew, and Katy

Contents

Illustrations

Preface

Great rivers hold an intriguing allurement for me. Like people, their personalities are changeable; but unlike people, a river can seem radically different at the same time, depending on the position from which one views it. Cold-hearted indeed is the individual who can gaze at a mighty river winding across the earth without feeling twinges of wanderlust. Certainly I can claim no such grasp of reality.

Of all the rivers that grace the North American continent, few have had as varied and significant a history as the Red River. Although less well known than others, such as the Mississippi and the Missouri, the Red has enjoyed a central position in the history of the American West. From the time of the arrival of Indians in North America to the present, some nation, state, or tribe has cherished the river for its advantages, claimed ownership of it, tried to discover the secrets it held, or tried to change it. From the beginning of the Franco-Spanish conflict in the Southwest to the end of the dispute between Texas and Oklahoma in the 1920s, the river was the center of controversy.

The idea of writing the history of a river is not new; myriad streams have served as the focal points for historical works. The approach used here is in some ways unique, however. Whereas previous studies have used the river to give unity to diverse events, this volume is the history of a river; only events that took place because of the river's presence are chronicled. For example, narration of the Red River War of the 1870s is omitted because that campaign was incidental to the existence of the stream. It received the river's name only because it took place nearby. Conversely, the Red River Campaign of the Civil War, the various missions of Athanase de Mézières, and the journey of Pedro Vial are included because the Red played a vital role in those events. In this manner I have not tried to write the history of the region but, rather, to write the story of how this river has had great economic, political, and social significance in a vast region of the American West.

The reader will note that the names of several Indian tribes that appear throughout this book may vary in spelling, usually as the result of European attempts to spell native names phonetically. The variations occur because of the different sound systems used, especially by Spaniards and Frenchmen, in the sources for this book. The passage of time sometimes led to spelling changes by the tribes themselves, also. I have taken the spellings from original sources where possible and have retained the variations for authenticity.

Some of the material for two chapters of the book has been published as articles. Chapter 7 was published as "Captain Randolph Barnes Marcy, 1849–1852," in *Frontier Adventurers: American Exploration in Oklahoma*, edited by Joseph A. Stout, Jr. It is used by permission of the Oklahoma Historical Society. Chapter 8 was published as "Highway of War," in the *Red River Valley Historical Review*, Volume III, No. 3, Summer, 1978. It is used by permission of the *Red River Valley Historical Review*. I gratefully acknowledge these courtesies.

Odie B. Faulk made helpful suggestions for the book, as did James H. Thomas, assistant professor of American Studies in Wichita State University. Both provided the friendship necessary to any writer. Finally, my wife, Toni, and my children, Jon, Matthew, and Katy have miraculously maintained their love for a grumpy husband and father and have suffered through long days and evenings while I worked on the manuscript. To them I owe the greatest debt.

CARL N. TYSON

LaVerne, California

The Red River in Southwestern History

1.

The River and Its People

To the weary pilgrim wending his way westward across scores of miles of changeless plains, the Rocky Mountains were a welcome change. Their massive peaks thrust skyward, some capped with eternal snow. This is the Continental Divide, separating the water that falls there and making it flow in two directions. On the western slope are two major rivers, the Colorado and the Columbia, while on the eastern side the Missouri, the Arkansas, and the Red have their headwaters. Of these the Red is the most southerly—and the one that spans the arid plains of the Southwest.

The Red River has no single source. It is born in the foothills of the Rockies from a thousand tiny rivulets. These come together on the Staked Plains—or, as the Spaniards named this region, the Llano Estacado,—the semiarid High Plains that slope gradually away from the Rockies, decreasing in altitude as they progress eastward. Although this land now is so flat that one can see for miles, its soil once was part of the peaks of the mountains, washed down by the rains of centuries past to form an alluvial plain. In the spring the short grama grass bursts into growth; as the ceaseless winds of summer blow, the grass tosses and tumbles like a green ocean. An occasional cottonwood tree dots the landscape to denote some small streambed that makes its way toward the Red River, while dwarf red cedars indicate the underground water near the surface.[1]

The Red crosses this Staked Plain that marks the panhandle of Texas. As it gathers strength from the tiny streams that flow into it, the river becomes broader and more stately, but everywhere its course winds and curves like the path of some giant snake. Because the Red has flowed through the plains for so long, it has cut deep into the surface—five to eight hundred feet in places—to form the Palo Duro Canyon, a region of canyon walls carved into myriad portraits and escarpments. From the bed of the river the walls seem to merge as they rise, creating the illusion that the river lies beneath a canopy of rock and sand.[2]

As the Red leaves the Llano Estacado, it flows into lower, broken country, eight hundred feet below the Staked Plains. Although some animals and plants, such as the prairie dog and the cottonwood, inhabit both areas, the plants and animals of the High Plains are more numerous and varied. Here the cottonwood is joined by the mesquite and the dwarf oak near surface water, and the prairie dog competes with jackrabbits and ground squirrels for available food. Larger beasts such as the cougar (or puma) and coyotes once wandered the land, searching for food and scattering smaller creatures in their wake. Here, too, roamed the American bison, a holdover from the days of saber-toothed tigers and mammoths. Woolly and tenacious, the buffalo had few enemies, for its size, strength, and ill temper discouraged all but the most determined predator. Only an occasional black bear could match the buffalo, and then only if the woolly bovine was alone.[3]

The buffalo inhabited the plains from the Canadian border to the Río Grande, moving with the weather and seeking fresh pasture. Because the herds had no natural predators and the land was plentiful, the buffalo multiplied quickly. When the first white men came to the American West, there were an estimated six million of these shaggy beasts in the southern herd. This herd grazed the plains of present-day Texas and Oklahoma, with the Red River providing a reliable water supply.[4]

The buffalo did not stay exclusively on the High Plains but

"Border of the El-Llano Estacado," a drawing from *Explorations of the Red River of Louisiana in the Year 1852*, by Captain Randolph B. Marcy and Captain George B. McClellan (Washington, 1854). Courtesy of the Western History Collections, University of Oklahoma Library.

wandered eastward in their eternal quest for grass. In this region the river changes as it flows off the Llano Estacado. The land is broken and sandy. No longer does the river cut deep and jagged banks; it meanders across the land, seeking the course of least resistance. With each freshening of the waters the river floods the surrounding country, widening its channel. Because the land is flat and soft, the river often forms "cutoffs" and rechannels its waters. The sandy bottom quickly becomes saturated with moisture, creating a deadly trap for any unsuspecting intruder.[5]

Some one hundred miles after it leaves the Llano Estacado,

the Red receives its first major tributary, the North Fork. This stream rises on the northeastern edge of the Staked Plains, on the southern side of the Canadian River watershed. It runs parallel to the Canadian before turning southward, making a long, gentle arc in reaching the Red. The North Fork is equal in size to the main stream, doubling the Red's burden at this confluence.[6]

A few miles above the juncture of the two branches the North Fork flows through the southwestern tip of the Wichita Mountains. These mountains, rising more than two thousand feet above the plains, are rich in minerals. Gigantic quartz deposits convinced early explorers that the mountains held riches of precious minerals, but the gold and silver that fortune hunters sought was present in only small amounts and would not be found until the twentieth century—and then not in paying quantities. Miners seeking copper, iron, and other useful metals would find scant success in the Wichitas. The minerals of the Wichitas served another purpose, however. For centuries water and wind eroded the earth in the hills, and the deposits were carried into the Red by Otter Creek, coloring the river. As a result the water was of a brownish, rusty tint; for this reason Spanish explorers named it Río Rojo (Red River).[7]

Ten miles before the North Fork enters, the river curves southward to cross the prairie that stretches from the Wichitas southward into central Texas. Moisture is abundant here, and the land is dotted with stands of cottonwood, oak, and various other plants. Beaver dams once gave silent evidence of their builders' presence. In the lush foliage that grows along the banks of the Red and its many tributaries, myriad animals make their homes and seek shelter from the elements and predators. Raccoons, foxes, and opossums burrow into the banks, waiting for darkness and their nightly hunts. Cottonmouth moccasins lie deadly in the grass by the waters, silently and patiently watching for an unwary frog. Overhead many species of multicolored birds chatter and screech their way through the branches and the sky.

In the countryside a covering of grass and bushes conceals a darting and scurrying world of cottontail rabbits, field mice, and other small creatures. Across the prairies once stalked predators of varying sizes and appetites, searching the land for food. Far above, lordly eagles and wary hawks soared, waiting for an incautious movement below to bring them plummeting to earth. A blundering visitor might be startled by the fluttering explosion of a disturbed covey of quail or awed by the beauty and grace of a fleeing antelope.[8]

After its junction with the North Fork the Red River flows almost due south, turning eastward at the mouth of the Pease River, which enters from the south. The Pease rises on the prairies of the lower Texas Panhandle, on the southeastern rim of the Llano Estacado. After gaining strength from the Pease, the Red then cuts eastward, reaching a confluence with Cache Creek near the ninety-eighth meridian. The latter stream rises on the southeastern slopes of the Wichita Mountains. Thus the Red collects the moisture from both sides of the Wichitas, from the North Fork and Cache Creek. Ten miles below the mouth of Cache Creek the Wichita River marries with the Red. The waters from these tributaries increase the river's burden greatly, creating a broad, turgid stream deep enough to support steamboat navigation.[9]

Twenty miles downstream the Red receives two additional major tributaries, Beaver Creek from the north and the Little Wichita River from the south. From here the Red continues eastward, gathering water of smaller streams such as Belknap, Farmers, Mud, and Walnut creeks. As it moves eastward from the ninety-eighth to the ninety-seventh meridian, the Red cuts a zigzag course, flowing north after its confluence with the Little Wichita, then dropping south, only to turn northward again to meet Walnut Creek. Near the mouth of Walnut Creek the Red River leaves the prairies and enters the Western Cross Timbers, a botanic and geographic phenomenon. In the midst of open country this massive stretch of trees and brush signals the beginning of a rough, broken country running from central Oklahoma southward to central Texas. In this area rolling hills and minor sandstone outcroppings give evidence of the Comanchean and Pennsylvanian formations on which it rests. Here the river changes also, reverting to a narrow channel with a sandy bottom. The course is better defined in this area, owing to the land's resistance to erosion and the inability of the stream to cut new channels with each freshening of the water.

As the Red enters the Western Cross Timbers, it turns southward, flowing in a southeasterly direction for about twenty miles before bending once again toward the east. At this point the river enters the Eastern Cross Timbers, which run along the ninety-seventh meridian. Similar to the western counterpart, the Eastern Cross Timbers consist of blackjack and post oak intermingled with mesquite and smaller shrubbery; however, the eastern stand of trees is generally taller and larger because of the more fertile land and greater rainfall. East of the Cross Timbers the land again is open prairie. Here the Black Prairie begins, so named because of the dark, rich tint of the heavy loam soil in the region.[10]

After leaving the Cross Timbers, the Red again becomes a broad, turgid stream, widening its bed with each new high water and creating new cutoffs. Because the soil is loosely packed and easily eroded, the river often flows into low areas during high water, cutting away the topsoil. This frequently results in the formation of multichannels, dividing the river's waters among several courses. At times high water washes away sufficient amounts of soil to create entirely new channels, a tendency that created myriad problems for surveyors and boundary commissioners.[11]

On the Black Prairie the Red receives its largest tributary, the Washita River. This stream also rises on the High Plains of the Texas Panhandle south of the Canadian's watershed; in-

"Gypsum Bluffs on North Branch Red River," a drawing from *Explorations of the Red River of Louisiana in the Year 1852*, by Captain Randolph B. Marcy and Captain George B. McClellan (Washington, 1854). Courtesy of the Western History Collections, University of Oklahoma Library.

deed, the headwaters of the Washita are less than twenty miles from the bed of the Canadian. From this source the Washita cuts a rough and meandering course to the southeast, entering the Red midway between the ninety-seventh and ninety-sixth meridians.[12]

East of the ninety-sixth meridian the land becomes broken and hilly. Long avenues of grassland are intermingled with patches of rolling hills. The land is fertile and green, and expansive stretches of timber denote a sharp increase in rainfall. Longleaf pines jut skyward into the moist air, casting their outsized cones into the breeze, thereby spreading their breed.

7

Giant live and white oaks stand majestically over the thickets of wild dewberries and poison ivy. Along the banks of the Red and its many tributaries in this region wildflowers grow in abundance. Bluebonnets, Indian paintbrushes, and sunflowers sprout from the sandy soil, tinting the terrain with bright blues, reds, and yellows; delicate honeysuckle hangs serpentlike across the shrubbery, scenting the breeze with sweetness and filling the mind with soft thoughts. Droopy willows bow demurely near surface water, and stately sycamores drop armored seedpods into the tall grasses beneath.

In this garden many animals once made their home. Wood bison, smaller cousins of the buffalo, grazed among the forests, petulant squirrels chattered in the branches, and mailed armadillos skittered warily about. The air was filled with unaccountable thousands of bothersome gnats and thirsty mosquitoes. The coo of feeding doves and the wail of the whippoorwill echoed across the land.

For almost two hundred miles past the mouth of the Washita, the Red courses eastward, gathering tributaries such as the Blue and Kiamichi rivers from the north and Bois D'Arc and Pine creeks from the south. Near the ninety-fourth meridian the river turns northward, starting its "Great Bend" to form a rough semicircle. On the northern arc of this half-moon the Little Red River enters. At the end of the bend the river flows southwest about ten miles, joining with Sulphur Fork near the boundary of the present-day states of Arkansas and Louisiana. From there the river flows southward more than fifty miles to receive the runofff from Caddo Lake, a shallow natural empoundment. The Caddo is fed by several streams that drain a large part of east Texas. Because of the heavy rainfall in this area the contribution of these streams increases the Red's burden measurably.

After passing Caddo Lake, the Red turns and flows at roughly a forty-five degree angle southeast toward the Mississippi. This land is almost tropical in climate. Huge cypress trees stand stately among the bayous along the river, with musky clumps of Spanish moss hanging among their branches. Rainfall is plentiful. Much of the land is inundated after spring and fall showers, drying only during the summer months. The winter is generally mild and short, the rest of the year invariably hot. During the wet months the air is oppressive with moisture and heat.[13]

As the Red flows through this area, it gathers water to form hundreds of swamps and bayous. The water in them is usually dark and brackish, providing an excellent breeding ground for mosquitoes. Snakes of every size and color glide across the surface. Olive-green bullfrogs croak in the lush grasses, and turtles sun themselves on logs or poke their heads periscope-fashion from the water. Eellike gars roll to the surface, showing their yellow undersides and scattering smaller fish in their wake. On the sandy banks of the Red lazy alligators once lounged in the sun or searched for anything edible.

Three hundred miles from the Gulf of Mexico the Red River reaches its destination—the Mississippi River. Here it empties its rusty contents into the greatest river of the North American continent, mingling its moisture with that from the Northern Rockies and the Appalachians—in short, with water from every state west of the Cumberland Gap and east of the Continental Divide. From the Llano Estacado to the Mississippi, the Red River flows more than twelve hundred miles, draining roughly one-tenth of the continent.[14]

This was the Red River as the white men found it, flowing ever toward the sea, moving for thousands of years before the Europeans ventured inland. But it did not flow unseen or unnoticed. Indians knew the benefit of living near an unfailing source of water. They also knew the advantage of waterborne transportation. They settled along the river to enjoy its bounty and sometimes to suffer its ill temper.

The lower Red River was the home of many of the Caddo Indians. This group included several different confederations related by common language and tradition. These were the Natchitoches, in present-day Louisiana; the Adais, just below the great bend of the river; the Eyeish Confederacy and the Kadohadacho Confederacy, along the river above the bend; and the Hasinais, west and south of the Eyeish Confederacy. The Caddos were woodland Indians, supporting themselves by hunting and cultivation. They tended various plants— corn, muskmelons, plums, cherries, grapes, and mulberries— all of which produced bountifully with little or no care; and they killed the game that inhabited the forests.[15]

The name Caddo was a contraction of Kadohadacho (Real Chiefs). Among the various tribes of the confederation the term Caddo was not applied by the Indians to all the different groups but was later broadened by white men as a convenient term for all the confederacies.[16]

The first contact between the Caddoan tribes and whites occurred during the march of Luis de Moscoso's column from Arkansas to Mexico. Moscoso, who had been DeSoto's lieutenant in Florida, found a group called the Amayes near the Red River in June, 1542. The next contact between Indians and whites occurred in 1687, when René Robert Cavelier, Sieur de la Salle, made his abortive journey toward Canada from south Texas. La Salle's attempt to settle Texas resulted in Spanish expansion into the area, and in the 1690s missionaries were sent from Mexico to the Caddos. Instead of promoting friendly relations between Spaniards and Caddos, however, the missionaries only alienated the Indians and drove them into the French camp. The Caddos were unwilling to accept the teachings of the padres, and the soldiers who accompanied the fathers continually molested Indian women. Unfriendly relations between Spaniards and Caddos would last through the seventeenth and eighteenth centuries.[17]

About 1700 the Caddos came under the influence of the French. At that time the sons of France were expanding their Louisiana colony up the Red River. In 1714, Louis Juchereau de St. Denis established a trading post on the Red River near the location of present-day Natchitoches, Louisiana. From there he conducted his expeditions in Spanish Texas. That was the beginning of a friendship between the French and the Caddos that would last until 1763 and the end of the Seven Years' War. Friendship with the natives would also play a vital role in French domination in the area until Spain gained ownership of it.

Upriver the Wichita Indians moved into the area west of the Kiamichi River and east of the Washita River about the turn of the eighteenth century. The Wichitas, including the Taovayas, Tawakonis, Yscanis, Wacos, and Kichais, had previously lived along the Arkansas River but had fled southward to escape the more warlike Comanche and Osage tribes who invaded the region. The Wichitas lived in permanent grasshut villages.[18]

Like the Caddos', the Wichitas' economy was based on hunting and agriculture. The Caddos and Wichitas generally maintained friendly relations because neither relied on conquest or looting for economic gain. The first contact with the Wichitas by whites was probably during the expedition of Francisco Vásquez de Coronado in 1541, when the tribe was living along the Arkansas. In 1719, Bernard de la Harpe visited a group of Wichitas living near the mouth of the Canadian River in present-day Oklahoma. From La Harpe's visit and subsequent trading between the French and the Wichita tribes the French gained the Indians' loyalty, an aid in their struggle with Spain for dominance of the region.[19]

West of the Wichitas lived the Lipan Apaches, an eastern branch of the large group of southern Athapascans who inhabited much of the Southwest. Nomadic and fierce, the Lipans warred with the Wichitas and the Caddos, enlarging their domain with each successful campaign. By the time of the coming of Europeans to the region, the Lipan Apaches had secured a stronghold extending from the Arkansas River southward through central Texas. Members of this group lived along the upper Red River until they were driven southward

11

by the Comanches in the first half of the eighteenth century. During this time the Lipan Apaches warred on three fronts: against the Comanches on the northwest, the Wichitas and Caddos on the east, and the Spaniards on the south.[20]

Unlike the Caddos and the Wichitas, the Apaches were not farmers. They were buffalo hunters. Because they followed the buffalo and based their economy on raiding, the Apaches were constantly at war with their neighbors; they needed room to stalk the buffalo and enemies to raid.[21]

West and north of the Lipan Apaches lived several tribes of the Comanche nation. The Comanches were the southern-most of the Shoshonean groups, having migrated from their ancient home in present Wyoming in the early part of the eighteenth century. The various Comanche divisions were semiindependent and banded together during wars. The principal subtribes along the Red River were the Nokonis (or Wanderers) who ranged from the Big Wichita River to the Llano Estacado, and the Quahadis (or Antelope People) who lived on the Llano Estacado. Members of another subtribe, the Kostsotekas (or Buffalo Eaters), sometimes ventured into the vicinity of the Red River from their homes along the Canadian.[22]

The Comanches, like the Apaches, lived by hunting buffalo and raiding other groups. Usually the Comanches limited their hostilities to the Apaches and to Spaniards and chose to ally themselves with the Kiowas on the north and the Wichitas on the east. Through their alliance with the Wichitas and because of their hatred for Spaniards, the Comanches were allies of the French who came into their territory from Louisiana.[23]

The Comanches were a proud and dignified people, looking on Spaniards as inferior. Trouble erupted because of the Spanish policy of attempting to missionize, educate, and Europeanize the natives. The Comanches believed that Spaniards had little to teach them and that their own way of life was infinitely superior. The result was a conflict of culture and arms, in both of which the Spaniards fared badly. The French made no attempts to change the Indians, but used them as allies against the Spaniards.[24] When whites came to the Southwest in the early part of the sixteenth century, they found the natives along the Red River living in harmony with nature and the river flowing wild and unfettered. Almost immediately the Europeans began to alter the way of life of the natives and to attempt to tame the great river and discover its secrets.

2.

The Struggle for Empire

The first Europeans to view the Red River were members of the expedition that Francisco Vásquez de Coronado led into west Texas in 1541. This group probably crossed the headwaters of the Red sometime in the early summer of that year on their way to conquer the Gran Quivira. During the return trip the disappointed conquistadors undoubtedly recrossed the stream, but these men were searching for gold and silver, not geographical knowledge. Thus the presence of the Red held little interest for them, other than as a supply of potable water—and yet another obstacle to cross. A year after Coronado crossed the Red, another Spaniard, Luis de Moscoso, led his party of fortune hunters from the east to the banks of the Red. This group also had little interest in the river, but it made its presence felt by delaying their march for a week because of high waters.[1]

Neither Coronado nor Moscoso had any interest in the region of the Red River, but their reports influenced the history of the area for centuries. Both had been in search of wealth—the Gran Quivira and the Seven Cities of Cíbola—and their failure to find riches pervaded their reports. To gold-hungry Spaniards the region was barren and worthless. Thus officials in Mexico and Spain found no reason to finance or organize further expeditions into the interior of North America. As a result the land along the Red River lay open and unclaimed, except for the grand Spanish assertion that the entire continent belonged to their king. Only the Indians walked the

14

land for 150 years after the first Spanish explorations. Then in the 1680s another country began coveting the region.[2]

In 1674, Père Marquette and Louis Jolliet descended the Mississippi River to the mouth of the Arkansas and then turned back to Canada after assuring themselves that the Mississippi flowed into the Gulf of Mexico. Their reports sparked a dream in the mind of a fellow Frenchman—René Robert Cavelier, Sieur de la Salle. La Salle envisioned a French post astride the mouth of the Mississippi River, dominating both the trade of the inland and the commerce of the Gulf of Mexico. His determination was sufficient for him to convince the king of France, Louis XIV, that his dream could be made a reality. In 1684, La Salle set out with a flotilla of four ships and about three hundred people to build his colony. Unfortunately La Salle and his colonists did not disembark at the mouth of the Mississippi; either because of poor navigation or by La Salle's design the party landed on the coast of present-day Texas and went ashore in January, 1685, at Matagorda Bay. La Salle's endeavors were ill-fated, whether or not he intended to land there. One ship had been lost to Spanish corsairs during the voyage, one was sent back to France, another was lost entering the bay to unload cargo, and the fourth returned posthaste to France. The colony was left without transportation—in an unfriendly land.[3]

Because of the loss of one vessel to the Spaniards, La Salle knew that Spanish officials would send parties to seek out and destroy his colony. He therefore moved his settlement away from the shore six miles up a tributary of the Lavaca River, probably Garcitas Creek. There the Frenchmen erected Fort Saint Louis, hidden away from the searching eyes of Spaniards. While the colonists began construction of a settlement, La Salle explored the countryside—and caused some latter-day observers to theorize that the Frenchman had purposely missed the Mississippi, perhaps to gain information about the Spaniards in Mexico, perhaps to be near the silver mines of Durango.[4]

La Salle's colony fared badly. Although the Indians in the area were friendly at first, they soon grew hostile to the Europeans. A war of attrition began, with the Indians the invariable winners. Meanwhile La Salle continued to explore the region. He made three exploratory journeys, one to the west, another to the north, and a third in search of the Mississippi. Finally, in January, 1687, La Salle decided that the colony needed outside help. Supplies had been exhausted, efforts to gather food had proved futile and dangerous, and the number of colonists had grown ever smaller because of the Indians. On January 12, 1687, La Salle and a small party of men set out for Canada. He hoped they would reach there in time to send back aid to the colonists left at Fort Saint Louis.[5]

After many days of hardship and privation members of the party reached Canada, but La Salle was not among them. He lay dead in the wilderness of east Texas, murdered by two of his own men—his dreams crushed by bad management, the elements, and poor planning. The survivors, led by Henri Joutel, La Salle's second-in-command, told of the plight of the colony and its founder. The French government and Louis XIV, however, were more interested in their affairs in Europe than in the fate of a small, seemingly worthless settlement in far-off North America.[6]

The Spaniards, in contrast, were not too busy to worry about La Salle. Immediately after word reached Mexico City of French colonization on the northwest shore of the Gulf of Mexico, which the Spaniards considered their private lake, expeditions were sent to destroy the settlement. But La Salle had hidden his colony well. All attempts failed until 1689, when Alonso de León found the fort with the aid of Jean Henri, a Frenchman who had left La Salle's settlement to become ruler of an Indian village in the area. They found the fort in ruins and most of the colonists dead. They heard rumors that most of the Frenchmen had been taken by the Indians, but fewer than a dozen were discovered among the natives.

Thus ended the French attempt to settle the coast of Texas; but the Spaniards were not satisfied.[7]

The viceroy of Mexico, the Condé de Galvé, realized that La Salle's colony in Texas might later be used to support a French claim to the area; he also knew that the colony could have been successful but for bad luck. Spain had to expand into Texas or risk a second French intrusion. The viceroy chose the former course. His task was made easier by the desire of a Spanish missionary, Father Damián Massanet, to missionize the Indians of east Texas. Massanet had accompanied Alonso de León during the search for La Salle's post, where he had met several Tejas Indians who appeared receptive to Christianity. Thus, when Galvé ordered De León back to Texas to destroy all remnants of the French post, Father Massanet was sent to build a permanent mission for the Tejas. That was accomplished in the spring of 1690. Father Massanet personally carried out the order and burned the remains of Fort Saint Louis. Then the Mission San Francisco de los Tejas was constructed on the banks of the Trinity River. Three Franciscan missionaries, including Massanet, were left to man the new mission while De León returned to Mexico to report their assignment completed.[8]

The viceroy, however, still feared that the French might successfully colonize Texas and threaten New Spain. In a classic example of defensive expansionism Galvé ordered the province of Texas formally settled. Captain Domingo Terán de los Ríos was appointed governor of the region, and Father Massanet was appointed superintendent of the missions of Texas. The results of these orders were disappointing. De los Ríos discovered that the Indians had turned hostile to the Spaniards at San Francisco de los Tejas, and that the missionaries had made little progress. He returned to Mexico early in 1692, leaving Massanet at the mission with a small company of soldiers.[9]

The situation at the mission grew rapidly worse. Droughts and epidemics, which the Indians blamed on the Spaniards,

17

created overt hostilities between Europeans and natives. Late in 1693 the viceroy decided to abandon the establishment; however, the missionaries, seeing a conflict between the work of God and their own welfare, had already decided to flee the mission. In October, 1693, the fathers buried their sacred ornaments and fled to Mexico. Once more Texas was left to the Indians.[10]

Shortly after Mission San Francisco de los Tejas was abandoned, Viceroy Galvé's fear that the French would encroach on Spanish territory was made real. During the period between 1693 and 1713 the French were busy. In 1699, Biloxi was founded in present-day Mississippi, and in 1702, Mobile was established in Alabama. By 1713 the French were ready to fulfill La Salle's dream of a French colony along the Mississippi. That year Louis XIV granted a monopoly for the colony of Louisiana to Antoine Crozat. Crozat named Sieur Antoine de la Mothe Cadillac governor of the colony. Cadillac was instructed to establish trade with the natives of the region and, if possible, with the Spaniards in Mexico. Although early attempts to trade with Mexico were rebuffed because of Spanish mercantile laws, Cadillac soon received an opportunity to initiate such trade.[11]

Early in 1713 he received a letter from the Franciscan missionary Francisco Hidalgo, who years before had been one of the padres at San Francisco de los Tejas. Hidalgo had longed to return to Texas, but his requests to do so had been denied repeatedly. In 1711 the padre turned to the French for help, writing to the governor of Louisiana to suggest that a joint missionizing project might successfully Christianize the natives of Texas. For Cadillac, Hidalgo's letter was a gift from heaven; he now had a reason to send a French agent into Spanish territory.[12]

Cadillac needed a talented and adventurous leader for his expedition into Mexico. The governor found an excellent individual in Louis Juchereau de St. Denis, the commander at

18

Biloxi. Cadillac decided that St. Denis should travel to the Río Grande to visit the Spanish outpost San Juan Bautista, where Father Hidalgo resided. All that was needed then was a route that would provide easy access to Texas and also take the Frenchmen among the Indian tribes along the way. The Red River fulfilled both requirements. This waterway was a natural choice for the French because of previous explorations of the river by their countrymen.[13]

In 1686, Henri de Tonty (or Tonti), who had been a member of La Salle's early Canada and Mississippi expeditions, had sailed down the Mississippi from the French colonies in Canada to search for La Salle. Tonty had been left in Canada when La Salle went to France to organize his expedition to colonize the mouth of the Mississippi and was to join the colonists after their arrival from France. Tonty's plans were changed, however, when he learned that the colonizing expedition had not landed at the Mississippi's mouth. When he failed to find the errant colony, Tonty had returned to Canada, but he had not given up hope of finding La Salle. Three years later he again voyaged down the Father of Waters; this time he sailed up the Red River, questioning the natives along its banks about the presence of other Frenchmen in the area. Tonty's search carried him far up the Red beyond the Caddo settlement near present-day Bayou Pierre. He then turned southward, reaching the Tejas Indians, who reported that Spanish soldiers had visited the area recently. They were the men of Alonso de León, who were also looking for La Salle. Because of rumors of Spaniards nearby and because of his failure to find any trace of his leader, Tonty retraced his path to the Red and down it, disappointed and discouraged. Back in the Illinois country, he found Henri Joutel and learned the sad news of La Salle's murder. Tonty's voyages had not been wasted, however; he had gained valuable information about the country along the Mississippi and Red rivers. He had also made contact with many Indians along the Red River and had begun a friendly relationship with the natives that would last until the end of French Louisiana and would prove invaluable to the French in their conflict with Spain in the region.[14]

Eleven years after Tonty's voyage in 1697, Jean Baptiste le Moyne, Sieur de Bienville, governor of Louisiana and a brother of the colony's founder (Pierre le Moyne, Sieur d'Iberville), explored the Red River and pushed across the entire breadth of present-day Louisiana. Bienville tried to reach the area in which La Salle had died, but spring rains and cold weather forced him to turn back. Although Bienville failed to reach his original goal, his trip was important. He rekindled friendly relations with the natives along the Red River, enhanced French knowledge of the region, and gave valuable experience to a young Canadian who accompanied him, Louis Juchereau de St. Denis.[15]

After returning from his explorations with Bienville, St. Denis commanded a post on the lower Mississippi from 1702 to 1705. He led several expeditions into the Indian country, including another visit in 1710 to the Indians along the Red River, when he traded with the Natchitoches and several other tribes of present-day east Texas. In 1712, St. Denis was appointed commander of the French settlement at Biloxi and was holding that office when Governor Cadillac chose him to lead the expedition into Spanish territory to discuss the possibility of a joint effort to missionize the natives of east Texas and to open trade between Louisiana and Mexico.[16]

In late September, 1713, St. Denis and a small group of traders left Mobile with a large quantity of trade goods. The party spent the winter of 1713–14 trading with natives along the Red River and in east Texas. St. Denis realized that if trade between the Spanish and French colonies was ever to become frequent and steady a post was needed midway between the Spanish settlements along the Río Grande and the French settlements along the Mississippi. Consequently he ordered a trading station constructed on the Red River and named it Natchitoches in honor of the Caddoan Indians who inhabited the surrounding area. After St. Denis won the allegiance of the natives with gifts and his personal charm, he established a headquarters for his travels and then set out for San Juan Bautista late in the spring of 1714. He arrived with his party at the Spanish settlement on the Río Grande early in the fall of the same year; there he presented his papers, including Father Hidalgo's letter, to the presiding commander, Captain Diego Ramón. When St. Denis inquired about the possibilities of commercial contact between the colonies of France and Spain Captain Ramón immediately arrested him and confiscated his trade goods. Unsure about what his next action should be, Ramón forwarded St. Denis's documents to the viceroy, the Duke de Linares, in Mexico City and placed the affable Frenchman under house arrest. While Ramón and St. Denis waited for a decision on the Frenchman's future to be made in Mexico City, the latter enjoyed the freedom usually granted a house guest rather than the restrictions of a prisoner. St. Denis used the time it took for the viceroy to respond to Ramón's questions to win the respect of his captors—and the heart of the commander's granddaughter, María Ramón. The Spaniards came to admire the gentle Frenchman for his gracious manners and sincere warmth.[17]

Six months after the Frenchman had arrived at San Juan Bautista, Captain Ramón was informed that the viceroy wanted St. Denis brought to Mexico City for questioning and appraisal. St. Denis left the Spanish outpost with a detachment of soldiers, ordering his men to return to Natchitoches and promising his newfound love that he soon would return. On St. Denis's arrival in Mexico City, he was questioned at length about the motives of the French in regard to Texas and the reasons behind his visit to Mexico. The adroit Frenchman replied that the sole interest of his country in the area west of Louisiana was the missionization of the natives and that his objective had been only to further that project. The viceroy remained suspicious of French intentions, however, and convened a council of war to decide what the Spanish reaction to

21

this new threat of French encroachment should be. The council reasoned that the French would not risk overt intrusion into territory that had already been settled and determined that a series of four missions should be constructed in east Texas to serve the Tejas Indians. Once more Spain would reach into Texas and attempt to tame the Tejas.[18]

The Spaniards moved quickly. Late in September, 1715, Domingo Ramón, the son of St. Denis's original captor and uncle of María, was appointed to lead the expedition. Ever enterprising and invariably alert, St. Denis secured an appointment as guide for this missionizing party by taking Spanish citizenship. St. Denis and the party then returned to San Juan Bautista, where he married María. Early in 1716 the party of sixty-five persons left the Spanish province of Coahuila. In addition to the soldiers, priests, and other official members of the expedition, María St. Denis journeyed northward into the wilderness with her new husband.[19]

With St. Denis acting as an interpreter and guide, the party reached the site of the abandoned Mission San Francisco de los Tejas in June of 1716. A new mission, Nuestro Padre de San Francisco de los Tejas, was built nearby. Father Francisco Hidalgo was appointed overseer of the new mission. Thus was fulfilled the desire he had expressed in his letter to the governor of Louisiana. His appointment, however, did not stop the chain of events that his letter had begun.[20]

Ramón's party traveled northward, leaving Hidalgo with his group of padres and two soldiers at the mission. They met several groups of Tejas, to whom St. Denis gave gifts. The natives received the Spaniards cordially and declared themselves subjects of the king of Spain. Three more missions, Purísima Concepción, San José, and Nuestra Señora de Guadalupe, were constructed among the Tejas. After fulfilling their orders, Ramón and St. Denis visited the French post at Natchitoches, where St. Denis was greeted by many of the men who had accompanied him to Mexico. From the post on the Red River the two men went to Mobile to discuss recent events

22

with the governor of Louisiana. At Mobile Ramón informed Governor Cadillac that, because Spaniards had undertaken to missionize the Indians of east Texas, there would be no need for further discussion of a joint effort by the two Catholic powers. Furthermore, because Spanish law prohibited trade between Louisiana and Mexico, officials in Mexico City could see no reason for future contact between the two colonies. As far as the Spaniards were concerned, the matter had ended.[21]

Despite Ramón's assertions and protestations, the French remained hopeful that officials in Mexico would permit commerce between the colonies. While Ramón was explaining to the governor that such a hope was futile, St. Denis was replacing the trade goods that had been confiscated two years previously. The Frenchman believed that he could overcome the legal obstacles to such trade because of his recently gained Spanish citizenship and his new family connections in Mexico. Ramón and St. Denis set out for east Texas when their respective tasks were completed, one seeking an end to his ordeal and the other looking forward to the beginning of a great enterprise. Both were disappointed by subsequent events.[22]

When they reached east Texas, they learned that two more religious establishments had been completed. St. Denis was dismayed to learn that San Miguel de Linares de los Adaes had been constructed only twenty-one miles from his post at Natchitoches. The Spaniards, wishing to ensure against further French encroachment, had built an establishment that would allow them to maintain a careful watch on their wily neighbors. Frenchman and Spaniard faced one another across the Red River.

Despite this setback St. Denis returned to San Juan Bautista, still hoping to sell or trade the goods he had acquired in Louisiana. The Spaniards, he theorized, might see things differently if he could demonstrate to them the advantages—and comforts—that trading with the French would bring. On reaching San Juan Bautista, however, he was arrested once again by Diego Ramón (now his grandfather-in-law). He was

23

told that it was equally illegal for Spanish citizens to bring foreign goods into Spanish colonies, and, for the second time, his goods were confiscated. Once more he was taken to Mexico City for questioning. There he pleaded ignorance of the law he had offended, and (on completion of that repeat performance,) he was again released from custody. His request to be allowed to return to Texas was denied, but he was given the money that had been gained from a public auction of his confiscated goods. Twice St. Denis had violated Spanish law, and twice he had talked his way to freedom. But he longed for his countrymen, and on September 5, 1718, he slipped away from Mexico City and returned to Natchitoches. Soon after his departure his bride joined him. It had been five years since his journey to Mexico had begun; during that time he had acquired a wife, had twice changed his nationality, and had twice been arrested. His actions had started a chain of events that culminated in the formation of a Franco-Spanish border along the Red River. He had triggered a conflict over control of the territory along that river that would last for more than four decades—for within a year of his return another remarkable Frenchman began trading along the waters of the Red River.[23]

3.

The Conflict Continues

Louis Juchereau de St. Denis returned to Natchitoches, but the talented Frenchman's career was far from over. After visiting the governor in Mobile and reporting the results of his escapades, St. Denis was appointed commander of the post he had founded on the Red River. He remained there with his wife for the rest of his life. Although the Spaniards at Los Adaes attempted to thwart his trading excursions into Texas, he exercised considerable influence over the local Indians, continued to trade freely with them, and extended the area controlled by his country.[1]

While St. Denis had been in Mexico, the official makeup of Louisiana had undergone a radical change. Antoine Crozat had lost more than two million livres while holding the commercial monopoly for Louisiana and in 1717 had returned the grant to the crown. The new king, Louis XV, had taken the purple on the death of his great-grandfather in 1715 and had been placed under the regency of his cousin, Philippe, Duke of Orleans, a brilliant nobleman. When the charter to Louisiana was returned, Philippe was approached by his close friend John Law, who had a scheme for the future of that territory in the New World.[2]

Law had fled to France from England, where he was wanted for killing a man in a duel over an affair of the heart. The exiled Englishman was a skilled promoter, a mathematical genius, and an inveterate gambler. While in France, he had already organized a highly successful bank with Philippe's blessings and had endeared himself to the regent. Law proposed that he be allowed to create a company for the administration of Louisiana, a company that he would control. On September 6, 1717, the Company of the West was chartered and held a monopoly for trade and colonization in Louisiana. The charter was for twenty-five years and included all the privileges that Crozat had previously enjoyed. In return, Law's company promised to send six thousand white settlers and three thousand black slaves to the colony within ten years. The Company of the West was capitalized at the fantastic amount of one hundred million livres. After arranging for the charter, John Law went to work selling stock at five hundred livres a share. A master of promotion, Law promised the people of France that within a matter of months the riches of Louisiana would swamp the entire nation with gold and silver from the mines and streams of the colony. France went speculation-mad.[3]

As the first shares sold, Law declared dividends—and the price per share was raised. Soon people were forming lines in the streets, demanding an opportunity to invest funds in Law's get-rich-quick company. Philippe d'Orleans was highly pleased with his friend's accomplishments and arranged for Law's private bank to serve as the Royal Bank of France. Through this bank Philippe made France a partner in the Company of the West.[4]

In the New World, Sieur de Bienville was appointed governor of Louisiana, a position he had held before Crozat's monopoly. Law's company decided that a city should be built astride the Mississippi near its mouth to make it forever a French stream. In September, 1717, orders were approved for the founding of New Orleans, a name chosen to honor the helpful regent. Three hundred "concessionaires" were named, and each was granted huge estates in Louisiana. In return the three hundred agreed to gain control of the area and extend French domain. Among the concessionaires who went to Louisiana in 1718 was Bernard de la Harpe.[5]

La Harpe had served in the French coast guard for more than five years before he received his concession in Louisiana. He was known as talented, loyal, and brash—the kind of man who attracted the attention of John Law and complemented that great speculator and his plan for Louisiana. Because of La Harpe's energetic and ambitious personality, his concession was situated in the contested territory—on the Red River.[6]

La Harpe arrived in New Orleans late in the fall of 1718. Although the city was little more than a few log buildings, the colony's government had already been established there. The Council of Louisiana, seeing an opportunity to spread French influence, appointed La Harpe commandant of the Nassonites, Kadohadachos, Nadocos, and Natchitoches Indians. All of these were Caddoan groups inhabiting the area around La Harpe's grant. His task was to secure their loyalty and trade. He also was ordered to explore the Red River and its tributaries, making contact with any natives in the area and bringing them under French influence. A trading post was to be established on the Red River, northwest of Natchitoches, and he was to renew efforts to open commercial routes with the Spaniards.[7] La Harpe departed for the Red River in December, 1718. With him went more than fifty traders, soldiers, and laborers, in a pair of large boats and a trio of smaller canoes. The trip to Natchitoches was unpleasant. High waters made movement upriver tedious and backbreaking, and cold weather made the travelers uncomfortable and ill. The party persevered, however, reaching the mouth of the Red early in January, 1719, and Natchitoches later the same month. There La Harpe met St. Denis, and the two adventurers discussed the possibilities of beginning trade with the Spaniards.[8]

Soon after his arrival La Harpe received the disturbing news that the Spanish governor of Texas, Don Martín de Alarcón, had ordered the establishment of a post on the Red River in the area of La Harpe's concession. La Harpe responded by notifying Alarcón of his presence and intentions. He then left for his grant on the Great Bend of the Red River. He arrived in that area early in the spring of 1719 and picked a location in present-day Red River County, Texas, because the "spot seemed to me very beautiful, having a beautiful coast spread toward the river." It was approximately two leagues above a Nassonite village on the river. Title to the location was obtained from a Nassonite chief for thirty pistols and a small quantity of merchandise. La Harpe immediately ordered construction of a log house to serve as a warehouse for the goods he had brought and a center for his future activities.[9]

Having established a headquarters on the Red, La Harpe began the task of winning the trust and loyalty of the neighboring natives. He easily gained the friendship of the Indians because he had brought great quantities of merchandise to be used as gifts, including firearms, which the Spanish refused the natives. At a massive meeting with the Nassonites, Caddaquions, Natsos, and Natchitoches, La Harpe gave gifts and promised to supply all their needs in the future. Sacred songs were sung, and vows of allegiance were exchanged during the festival, which lasted twenty-four hours. Afterward La Harpe ordered a blockhouse for trade goods to be built at the Nassonites' village.[10]

La Harpe initiated contact with the Spaniards in east Texas, hoping to open trade. He wrote Father Margil, the Franciscan missionary in charge of the Spanish missions of east Texas, suggesting that Margil cooperate with the French in securing illegal trade with the Indians and Spaniards of Texas in return for a liberal commission on sales made through the priest's cooperation. Margil responded favorably. Thus French commercial influence was extended into the lands under Spanish occupation.[11]

In May, 1719, La Harpe received a reply to his correspondence with Governor Alarcón of Texas. The Spaniard noted that he was somewhat surprised by the presence of Frenchmen among the Nassonites; surely, he wrote, La Harpe must realize that they and their lands belonged to Spain. The Nassonites, Alarcón asserted, were under Spanish control because they came under an extension of settlements in New Mexico. Oddly, Alarcón did not note either the explorations of Captain Terán de los Ríos in the 1690s or the missionary activities in east Texas as points that supported Spanish claims. La Harpe replied that the governor was mistaken and delineated the foundation of French claims to the Nassonites. He asserted that, because the post was on the Red River, a tributary of the Mississippi, it belonged to France. Frenchmen had explored and settled the Mississippi, and it and all its tributaries were French domain. Thus it was the Spaniards, not the French, who were the usurpers. The province of Texas was part of Louisiana because of Sieur de la Salle's settlement and because of other actions that La Harpe noted but failed to specify. Finally, the Frenchman responded to Alarcón's warning that La Harpe should vacate Spanish territory or face physical expulsion by suggesting that the Spaniard come and try. It was understandable that the undermanned Spaniard declined La Harpe's offer.[12]

Having secured the friendship of the local natives, opened trade with them and with Spaniards in east Texas, and established French dominion over the Great Bend of the Red River, La Harpe set out to explore the territory upriver from his post. Because he wished personally to explore the region north of the Red, he sent the Sieur du Rivage with an expedition westward on the Red. He instructed Du Rivage to make contact with the "roving bands" who lived along the river's course. To ensure ready friendship, Du Rivage carried with him a large number of gifts for the natives he hoped to meet. He was instructed to learn the location of the nearest Spanish settlement, the distance to New Mexico, and all information concerning neighboring natives. If possible Du Rivage was also to make an alliance with these roving nations. These tribes, La Harpe perceived, would make excellent allies because of their proximity to New Mexico.

Du Rivage set out early in the summer of 1719.[13] With him went four soldiers, six French traders, and eight Indian warriors. The Indian warriors were to serve as interpreters and guides. While traveling along the banks of the Red River, Du Rivage encountered several groups of roving nations, including the Kichai (Quidehais), Naouydiches, Joyuan, Huanchane, Huane, and Taovaya bands, all branches of the Wichitas. The Frenchmen were greeted cordially by these groups, who declared their friendship for the Europeans. They were happy to receive the French because of the continuing hostilities they were engaged in with the Lipan Apaches who lived west on the river. Du Rivage learned that the Wichitas had recently returned from a clash with the Apaches, whom he called "Cancys." This recent battle had ended in victory for the Wichitas, although the Apaches were receiving aid from the Spaniards.[14]

Du Rivage learned that for seventy leagues west of the Nassonites the various bands of Wichita Indians were masters of the land. The Apaches, however, had been expanding continually eastward. At that time the Apaches had accepted aid from Spaniards because of the invasion of their lands by the Comanches. The Spaniards unwisely had refrained from giving the Apaches firearms, although they had provided them with good horses, swords, and other equipment, which gave them an advantage over the Wichitas.[15]

Du Rivage learned that sixty leagues west of the Kichai village, where he had parlayed with the various Wichita chiefs, the Spaniards had mined some kind of precious metal. He was also told that the area along the Red River was heavily populated with Lipan Apaches. The Wichitas had pursued the Apaches as far as their villages on the Red, but the Spaniards had forced them to retreat from the pursuit by using cannon. After completing his task, Du Rivage returned to La Harpe's post, taking two Kichai warriors with him to act as guides for La Harpe's journeys north of the Red River.[16]

Before La Harpe was ready to depart on his explorations, he received the disturbing news that war had broken out between Spain and France. La Harpe, "seeing that the war was an obstacle to commerce that I had attempted to make with the Spanish and that I had nothing to fear from them for the present at my post, and thought it would be of interest," set out to explore the region north of the Red River.[17] His travels carried him to the mouth of the Canadian River, where he was told that Spanish settlements in New Mexico could be reached by way of the Arkansas River.[18]

The war that precipitated La Harpe's excursion had begun in Europe. A quarrel between the Bourbon monarchs over the island of Sardinia had turned to open conflict. Although the conflict ended quickly and indecisively in Europe, it changed the course of events in the New World. The French at Natchitoches received word of the conflict before their Spanish counterparts at Los Adaes learned of it. The military commander at the French post, Corporal M. Blondel, led a small party across the Red toward Los Adaes, hoping to extend French influence. The Spaniards, hearing the news of war and a French advance, beat a hasty retreat from their posts in east Texas. Blondel, in one movement, had secured east Texas for France.[19]

Although Blondel's coup appeared to swing the advantage to France, many persons in Louisiana disapproved of his action. Spaniards almost certainly would attempt to reassert themselves in east Texas; also, French control of the area was not entirely advantageous to the Frenchmen of Louisiana. Indeed, when La Harpe returned from his explorations, he was shocked to learn of Blondel's forceful actions. The removal of the Spaniards from Los Adaes would decrease his profits. If the Spaniards remained in San Antonio, La Harpe's contraband trade would cease. The unfortunate Blondel was forced to write a humble letter to the frightened padres to ask their gracious forgiveness for his most inappropriate actions and to beg them to return to their missions in east Texas.[20]

Despite the restoration of peace between Spain and France and Blondel's act of contrition, Spanish officials in Mexico were determined to prevent a recurrence of the fiasco. They decided that east Texas had to be resettled with a force large enough to preclude any future French intrusion. A willing leader for the expedition was found in the Marqués de Aguayo, a wealthy resident of the province of Coahuila. Previously he had sought the opportunity to settle Texas. Officials in Mexico had not found his plan suitable; however, after the affair of 1719, he was granted his request.[21]

In 1720, Aguayo led five hundred men into east Texas. The missions and their presidial partners were to be reoccupied. Any resistance, French or Indian, was to be crushed. Such a large force was entirely unnecessary. The French sincerely desired a Spanish return to the missions around Los Adaes—at least for the present. St. Denis met the Spaniards at the Neches River, greeting them as old friends. The French had withdrawn from east Texas to Natchitoches, and St. Denis had asserted his influence over the natives to smooth the Spaniards' return to Los Adaes. The Spaniards remained unconvinced of the Frenchman's sincerity, as well they might.[22]

After greeting the Spaniards, St. Denis journeyed to Mobile to report their arrival to Governor Bienville. The governor had opposed the return of Spaniards, but had been overruled by officials of the Company of the West, who were more desirous of gaining commercial profits than of controlling territory. Aguayo rebuilt the missions and presidios of east Texas, and by 1721 his task was completed. Los Adaes was rebuilt, and once again Spaniards and Frenchmen faced each other across the Red River.[23]

When Spanish officers visited the French settlement at Natchitoches, they were received cordially. They asserted that the reoccupation of Los Adaes was merely a return to the status quo of 1719, not an act of aggression. In turn the French promised to refrain from any overt act of war. Furthermore, La Harpe, who had argued in writing in 1718 that the boundary of Louisiana extended to the Río Grande and New Mexico, acknowledged the rights of Spaniards west of the Red River, thereby bowing to commercial pragmatism.[24]

32

In 1720, while Spaniards and Frenchmen juggled the boundary along the Red River, the Company of the West collapsed. Its founder and director, John Law, fled France, for his bubble had burst. Although the company continued for nine years after its financial breakdown, Louisiana was divided into nine judicial districts, ranging from New Orleans to Illinois and from Arkansas to Mobile. A council was created to oversee the affairs of the colony. Thus the efforts of La Harpe and St. Denis to reap the benefits of commerce for the company were ended, but the conflict along the Texas-Louisiana frontier continued.[25]

Spaniards had accepted the presence of Frenchmen in Louisiana, but they had not admitted any French right to possession of the province. Following the War of the Spanish Succession, Spain's policy had been to permit French presence as a buffer to the English colonies along the Atlantic seaboard. This policy of winking at French encroachment in Louisiana extended only to existing settlements. The policy in Madrid and Paris was to ignore each other's New World colonies. However, that was not the policy in Mexico City or New Orleans, and certainly it was not the policy along the Red River.[26]

The year after the failure of the Company of the West, La Harpe traveled again into the region north of the Red River, attempting to open a route to New Mexico. The frontier remained relatively quiet for several years. Indeed, in 1727, Don Pedro de Rivera made a tour of the east Texas missions and presidios. As a brigadier in the Spanish army Rivera was to inspect the area and make suggestions. He believed that Spaniards were secure on this northern frontier and suggested sharp decreases in the number of soldiers stationed there. In 1735 the frontier again became unsettled when the French moved the post of Natchitoches a short distance westward. The move was made to escape the flooding of the Red River, which frequently inundated the settlement. In carrying out this move, St. Denis believed the French to be entirely within

33

their rights. The area that lay along the Arroyo Hondo, a small tributary of the Red, had for many years been considered French domain because France had controlled the several ranches dotting the region. The Spanish reaction was surprisingly firm. José Gonzales, the lieutenant governor of Texas, declared that the move was a breach of the unspoken contract that had regulated the frontier since the confusion of 1720. Accordingly he voiced his protest to St. Denis and informed his own superior, Governor Juan Manuel Sandoval, of the seeming French aggression. The governor, who evidently felt that the time had come for a hard policy, ordered his aide to command the French to remove their offending post. Gonzales was ordered to repeat the demand three times. If the French ignored this admonition, they were to be expelled forcibly.[27]

St. Denis was neither terrorized by Gonzales's threats nor impressed by the Spanish claim to the area west of the Red River. He knew that the limited number of Spanish soldiers in Texas precluded physical expulsion. The talented Frenchman had answers for both Spanish threats and claims. He informed Governor Sandoval that neither country could legitimately claim the area between Los Adaes and Natchitoches. When Governor Sandoval realized that St. Denis would not evacuate to the original location of Natchitoches short of overt hostilities, he referred the affair to officials in Mexico City. That action effectively ended the dispute; questions asked in Texas rarely brought answers from Mexico City. Natchitoches remained at its new location.[28]

Although the dispute between St. Denis and Sandoval ended in a tactical victory for the Frenchman, the Spaniard had the final word. Either out of anger at St. Denis's obstinancy or because of his determination to stop French commercial encroachment, the governor decreed that all trade between Texas and Louisiana should cease. Clandestine commerce continued after Sandoval's proclamation, but overt trading was discontinued, creating severe shortages in Natchi-

Caddo Indian village showing grass-thatched houses similar to those seen by early explorers of the Red River. Courtesy of the Western History Collections, University of Oklahoma Library.

toches. Spanish enforcement had become so lax that the French had become dependent on Los Adaes for supplies. Another result of the affair was of more lasting importance. In recognition of an accomplished fact the two commanders thereafter observed the Arroyo Hondo as the boundary between their colonies.[29]

While St. Denis and Sandoval had been arguing over the boundary between Louisiana and Texas, another struggle had been taking place—one for control of the various Indian tribes who lived along the contested border and the Red

River. The natives of the region were the key to control of the country. Neither the French nor the Spaniards were able or willing to garrison a sufficient number of men along the Red River or in the surrounding area to dominate the other. Also, neither were able to colonize the area along the common border and overwhelm the other. Both were thus forced to rely on the Indians as allies and to attempt to create alliances strong enough to compel the opposing nation to give up the struggle.[30]

While the Spaniards were striving to break the Caddos' allegiance to France, the French were moving to bolster their own position. The same year that Margil was sent to east Texas, a group of Caddoan Indians, the Yatasis, were moved down the Red and settled among the Natchitoches. This move further enhanced the French position and precluded any Spanish efforts among those tribes. The establishment by La Harpe of Nassonite Post among the Indians of that name was the final act in the struggle for the allegiance of the Caddos. The post effectively ended any Spanish expansion into the area along the Red River from the Great Bend to its mouth. That length of the river was French.[31]

With La Harpe among the upper Caddoan tribes and St. Denis among their counterparts downriver, there was no chance for Spanish encroachment after 1719. This situation was enforced by the presence of St. Denis at Natchitoches from the time of his return from Mexico until his death in 1744. Like a father St. Denis watched over the Caddos and ensured their allegiance to France.[32]

West of the Caddos, the Wichita Indians remained aloof from the struggle until the coming of La Harpe to the Great Bend of the Red River in 1719. The first European visitor to the Wichitas was probably Sieur du Rivage, who came during the explorations that had been ordered by La Harpe. Du Rivage established friendly relations with the Wichitas by liberally distributing gifts. He found several of the Wichita tribes living on or near the Red River; also, he found them at war with the Lipan Apaches. Further French contact with the Wichita tribes was made that same year by La Harpe. He traveled northward into present-day Oklahoma, meeting several subtribes of the Wichitas at a great convocation near the mouth of the Canadian River. There he presented many gifts to the natives and promised to return often with trade goods. Because the Indians needed firearms and because they cherished the shiny manufactured goods that La Harpe showed them, they quickly proclaimed their love for France. Sacred songs were sung, and the peace pipe was passed. In return for the presents La Harpe had brought and in demonstration of their friendship, the natives treated him like a king and made him presents of salt, ultramarine, and an Apache slave. The Indians' departure for their annual hunt ended La Harpe's plan to establish a trading post at the site of the gathering, but the Frenchman did raise the royal ensign of France there to remind the natives of their French friends.[33]

Two years after his first trip to meet the Wichitas, La Harpe attempted to ascend the Arkansas River to the location of the Wichita villages near the site of present-day Muskogee, Oklahoma. Though he was prevented from attaining his goal by low water and illness among his men, he did meet several Wichita Indians and rekindled his friendship with them. Thus the French laid the basis for a strong friendship with the Wichitas.[34]

All the activities of the French among the Wichitas, however, were needless. The Spaniards in Texas and New Mexico virtually forced the Wichitas to become allies of the French, although Spanish contact with the tribe was almost nonexistent. The reasons were twofold. First, the Wichitas were shielded from the Spaniards in Texas by their enemies the Lipan Apaches and from the Spaniards in New Mexico by the Comanches. Second, Spaniards appeared to ally themselves frequently with the Apaches. As demonstrated by the events that took place during Du Rivage's and La Harpe's explorations, the Apaches and the Wichitas were constant and bitter enemies. Thus the Spanish alliance with the Apaches forced the Wichitas to turn to the French for aid.[35]

After the early visits by La Harpe and Du Rivage to the Wichitas, trade between the natives and the French continued unabated until the cession of Louisiana to Spain in 1762. The extent of French influence over the Wichitas was indicated by Governor Kerlerec of Louisiana, who wrote in 1753 concerning the Wichitas and the Caddos, "They all agree unanimously in recognizing the French Governor of Louisiana as their father, and they never deny his wishes in the least." Also, as early as the 1720s the fleur-de-lis was flying over Wichita villages along the Red and Arkansas rivers as symbols of the solidarity between the French and the Wichitas.[36]

This alliance with the Wichitas proved highly useful to the French. It negated any chance of Spanish encroachment, and it provided a reliable and profitable source of raw products, such as furs, salt, and ultramarine. But the most important aspect of the alliance was the contact that it provided between the French and the Comanches. The Comanches were the most powerful Indian nation along the Red River and were a nominal ally of the Wichitas because of their mutual hatred of the Lipan Apaches. Through the Wichitas the French were introduced to the Comanche tribes living on the upper Red. The result was a triple alliance, with the Wichitas in the middle holding the other two together. Through this alliance the French were able to dominate the entire length of the Red River, with the exception of a short stretch between the Wichitas and the Comanches, which the Lipan Apaches controlled.[37]

The friendship of Comanches and the Wichitas enhanced the value of the latter tribe as a source of trade goods. After 1720 the French supplied the Wichitas with firearms which they subsequently traded to the Comanches—heightening their already awesome military prowess. In return for these weapons the Comanches traded horses, mules, and gold taken from Spaniards in New Mexico and Texas. The Coman-

"Wichitaw Village on Rush Creek," a drawing from *Explorations of the Red River of Louisiana in the Year 1852*, by Captain Randolph B. Marcy and Captain George B. McClellan (Washington, 1854). Courtesy of the Western History Collections, University of Oklahoma Library.

ches also exchanged Indian slaves, who were mostly Lipan Apaches, with the Wichitas. The Wichitas then traded the horses, mules, and slaves to the French in Louisiana for more firearms and other supplies, ending one cycle of the trading circuit and beginning another. This commercial alliance was beneficial to all the groups involved; but it was highly detrimental to the Spaniards and the Apaches.[38]

In addition to the advantages they provided in commercial ventures, the Wichitas and Comanches were strong military allies of the French, as demonstrated by events in the late 1750s. For many years the Comanches had been pressing the

Apaches from the north, driving them southward into the settled areas of Spanish Texas. The Apaches, in turn, had raided isolated Spanish towns. The Spaniards had reacted by attempting to missionize the Apaches and bring them under Spanish influence. These attempts had been futile until 1757, when the Apaches asked for a mission to be built for them on Río San Sabá in present-day west Texas. Hard pressed by the Comanches, the Apaches hoped to secure some relief by directing the Comanches' attention to the Europeans. The Spaniards, for their part, believed that this mission would prevent a French expansion toward New Mexico, stop Apache raids on Spanish settlements, and create a buffer area between the Comanches and themselves. In the spring of 1757, Mission San Sabá de Santa Cruz was constructed on the Río San Sabá, near present-day Menard, Texas. Father Alzonso Giraldo de Terreros was placed in charge. An accompanying presidio, under the command of Colonel Diego Ortíz de Parrilla, was built about two miles upriver from the mission. The Apaches did not settle at the mission, however; in June of that year three thousand of them passed by the establishment, saying that they had to hunt the buffalo but promising to return afterward. The Apaches realized that the Spaniards had announced their friendship by constructing the mission, and by doing so they incurred the enmity of the Comanches and their allies. The Apaches were waiting to see what the Comanches' reaction to the mission would be. The answer came in March, 1758.[39]

During the winter of 1757–58 the padres at Mission San Sabá heard rumors that the Comanches planned to destroy the settlement. On March 2 the presidial herd was stolen, and Colonel Parrilla tried to persuade the fathers to flee to the presidio for safety. The padres refused. A fortnight later, on the morning of March 16, two thousand Comanche warriors approached the mission and demanded a letter from Father Terreros that would give them admittance to the presidio. It was understandable that the father complied, and the Indians rode off in the direction of the presidio.[40]

After reaching the fort at midmorning, the Indians presented the letter to Colonel Parrilla—who, not surprisingly, refused to admit them. Thwarted by his refusal, the natives returned to the mission to avenge their setback. The Indians massacred the entire company except nine Spaniards who barricaded themselves in a room at the mission. The Comanches then left, taking what they could carry, after setting fire to the establishment. That night Parrilla sent a scouting party, who found four of the men who had hidden inside the mission still alive. Parrilla immediately reported the massacre to the viceroy in Mexico City.

The viceroy called a council of war, and in the latter part of June, 1758, the council determined that the Comanches should not go unpunished for their transgression. Mission San Sabá was to be reestablished, and a force under the command of Colonel Parrilla was to march northward to chastise the offending natives. But the reasons behind this expedition went deeper than merely punishing the Comanches. Spanish honor had been offended, and failure to punish the Comanches would embolden other natives to rise up in rebellion. No Spaniard would be safe on the northern frontier. Colonel Parrilla was ordered to raise a force sufficient to defeat the Comanches in armed conflict.[41]

By August, 1769, Parrilla was at San Antonio with a force of more than five hundred men, whom he had recruited wherever possible. Among the men he had gathered were a few trained soldiers. Most were merchants, tradesmen, and laborers, however, hardly a force capable of overwhelming the war-wise Comanches. Parrilla hoped that numbers would bring him victory. In addition, he was accompanied by more than a hundred Apache volunteers, who hoped to gain vengeance on their hated enemy.

Leaving San Antonio in August, the party marched northward in search of the enemy. For more than three hundred miles Parrilla pushed on with no sight of the Comanches until he reached the Red River, near present-day Ringgold, Texas. There, at a Wichita village, Parrilla found the enemy in a palisaded fort, surrounded by a moat, with the French flag flying above it. [42]

At that time Spain and France were allies in Europe. Along the Red River they were enemies. With the aid of French advisers the Comanches and their allies had constructed a European-style fort. Although surprised and dismayed by what he found, Parilla ordered his force to attack. The artillery brought by the expedition was called into play, but the natives had constructed their fortress well. The shells had little effect. Parrilla later reported that the Indians greeted each blast with shouts of laughter. Dutifully Parrilla ordered a charge. The Comanches, armed with modern weapons, easily rebuffed the assault. Parrilla then encamped for the night, hoping for some miracle that would bring him victory. That evening the colonel learned that the enemy was attempting to encircle his position to cut off his route of retreat. Also the garrison inside the fort was growing in number as more Indians arrived. Some of Parrilla's soldiers had already deserted, as had the entire force of Apache volunteers. The only recourse was to retreat to San Antonio. The cannon were left for the Indians. The march southward was marked by repeated Comanche attacks on stragglers, as well as on the main body. The expedition to avenge Spanish honor ended with another blemish on Colonel Parrilla's record. [43]

The defeats at Mission San Sabá and Spanish Fort, as the Wichita village on the Red became known, were never avenged. Four years later news reached the area that all of French Louisiana had been ceded to Spain during the settlement of the Seven Years' War, a conflict that ended in tragedy for both Spaniards and French. France lost most of its possessions in North America, while Spain lost Florida to the English. In payment for the loss of Florida and to preclude a Brit-

Commanche Indian encampment near Fort Sill in 1890. Earlier tipis were made of animal skins; later canvas tipis retained the same type of construction. Courtesy of the Western History Collections, University of Oklahoma Library.

ish seizure, France gave the Louisiana territory to Spain. The Red River no longer marked a boundary, for the Mississippi now separated Spanish and foreign territory.[44]

During the years of French ownership of Louisiana, the Red River had played an important role in their domination of the region. It not only served as an international boundary but also gave the French the upper hand in the struggle to open trade with the Spaniards. Because the Red stretched from the Mississippi, in the heart of Louisiana, to the country of the Caddos, Wichitas, and Comanches, it acted as a tie between these natives and the French. The river provided a natural highway for commerce between the natives and French Louisiana. The Spaniards in Texas were connected with the Indians on the plains by endless miles of hostile country that discouraged all but the most determined travelers. Commerce between the natives and Spaniards had proved expensive and sporadic. Thus the Red River had helped the French win the loyalty of the Indians of the region. France had lost Louisiana on the battlefields of Europe and the Atlantic seaboard, but not along the Red River.

4.

Spain and the Red River

The province of Louisiana, French for more than six decades, suddenly became Spanish in 1763. From Mobile to Natchitoches, from New Orleans to Chickasaw Bluffs, loyal citizens of France were transformed into subjects of Spain by the signing of a treaty in Europe. Thousands of Indians scattered across the extensive territory were suddenly made allies of Spain. Many of these natives had been taught by the French for years that Spaniards were the enemy—an enemy to be used, cheated, robbed, and sometimes fought. The new owners of Louisiana inherited the task of pacifying both Frenchmen and Indians.

Fortunately for the Spaniards, many of the French residents of Louisiana were apathetic about the ownership of the land they inhabited and were willing to aid their new landlords. Because of the experience that the French frontiersmen had had in dealing with the Indians, their aid was considerable. And because of the Indians along the Red River, living between the valuable commercial outposts of Natchitoches and Santa Fe, relations with these natives were crucial to Spanish success in the New World. These tribes, the Caddos, Wichitas, and Comanches, were traditional enemies of Spain. Luckily the Spaniards found a capable man willing to placate the quarrelsome natives—Athanase de Mézières.[1]

When Louisiana was ceded to Spain, Christophe Athanase Fortunat de Mézières was a captain at Natchitoches. The son of a well-to-do couple, Louis Christopher and Marie An-

45

toinette Clugny de Mézières, he had come to Louisiana in 1733, had established himself as a talented soldier and Indian agent, and had become successful in various commercial ventures. About 1740 he had moved to Natchitoches. During the years between 1740 and 1763 he had risen steadily through the ranks. Under Governors Bienville, Vaudreuil, and Kerlerec he had maintained official favor. He had also won the respect and friendship of Louis Juchereau de St. Denis. In 1746, two years after that already-legendary figure's death, De Mézières had married María Petonille Feliciana Juchereau de St. Denis, the daughter of Louis and María St. Denis. Unfortunately, De Mézières's young wife died in 1748.[2]

The cession of Louisiana precipitated De Mézières's premature retirement; he was discharged on September 15, 1763. Little is known of his activities immediately after his retirement other than that he remained in Natchitoches. He must have been restless, for in 1769, when Spanish officials were looking for a replacement for Baltazar de Villieis, another Frenchman who had been retained as commander of Natchitoches, De Mézières quickly accepted the position. He was appointed lieutenant governor of Natchitoches by Governor Alejandro O'Reilly. It mattered little that the French lilies had been replaced by the Spanish castle and lion; Athanase de Mézières would utilize his considerable skills and experience to ensure a smooth Spanish administration in Louisiana and amicable relations with the natives along the Red River.[3]

Since the establishment of French Louisiana, the trade in mules, horses, and slaves along the Red River had been a thorn in the side of Spanish officials in Texas and New Mexico. This commerce had ended the French demand for these articles in Louisiana and had created bonds between them and the Indians. Only the Spaniards, from whom the Indians stole the commodities, had suffered. To De Mézières fell the task of stopping this trade—and keeping the tribes content.[4]

Immediately after receiving his appointment, De Mézières began arranging for a meeting with the natives who lived along the Red River. He hoped that such a conference would remove most of the problems between Spain and the Indians. Before the meeting could be held, Governor O'Reilly, an alien in the service of Spain and strong supporter of De Mézières, was replaced by Luis de Unzaga y Amezaga. The new governor was leery of both the natives and De Mézières, and he delayed granting permission for the gathering. On September 20, 1769, after almost four months of admonitions from De Mézières, Unzaga y Amezaga agreed but warned the Frenchman to "make sure that the peace which they [the Indians] ask is single-minded, pure, and free from any criminal machinations."[5] De Mézières quickly consolidated his plans to meet with the tribes.[6]

When the Spaniards took control of Louisiana, they prevented French traders from visiting the Caddo and Wichita villages on the Red River. The natives had come to rely on European goods and began to raid Spanish outposts in retaliation. Although the traders had been allowed to resume their travels, the tribes had remained troublesome. The primary purpose of De Mézières's conference was to stop the raids.[7]

Following the Red River, the Frenchman and his party traveled to the village of the Caddochos in the early fall of 1770. The site was about one hundred Spanish leagues above Natchitoches on the river. With De Mézières went soldiers from both Natchitoches and the Spanish outpost Los Adaes. The mixture of members in the party was designed to demonstrate the solidarity of the Spanish provinces of Texas and Louisiana. A Franciscan, Father Miguel Santa María y Silva, was also selected to join the mission in order to impress on the tribes that priests of the same order in Texas should be treated with respect. This message was especially directed at the Wichitas who had taken part in the raid on the mission at San Sabá in 1758, in which two Franciscans had been killed.[8]

At the Caddocho village the Europeans were greeted by Chief Tinhioven, who welcomed them to his home. He proposed to act as a mediator between De Mézières and the other

47

tribes. When some chiefs of the Wichitas arrived De Mézières learned that many others had turned back because they suspected the meeting to be a trap. Those who came noted that they also expected punishment but asserted that their valor had overcome their trepidations.[9]

When those present were gathered, De Mézières noted that in the past the tribes had committed abuses on the Spaniards that were "worthy of eternal silence since with remembrance of it alone one's eyes were filled with tears."[10] But those times had passed, and France had left Louisiana forever. He warned that the Spanish king was the mightiest monarch on earth and that the natives were in danger of incurring his terrible wrath if they did not cease their warlike ways. If they did cease such ways, the king would forgive their past transgressions. Peace and friendship would reign. De Mézières also noted to the Wichitas that their position was unenviable, for they were surrounded by enemies and potential enemies from whom only the Spaniards could protect them.[11]

The leaders of the offending tribes were conciliatory. The Wichitas argued that their tribe had become enemies of the Spaniards because the Europeans had befriended the hated Apaches and that they were now ready for peace. But, they warned, the Comanches were irritated that the chiefs had counseled with the Spaniards and had begun hostilities, sorely pressing their tribe's existence.[12]

De Mézières admitted that he was sympathetic to the Wichitas' position but demanded that they travel to San Antonio, the site of many of their depredations, to make peace with the commander there. The Wichitas demurred at this suggestions, asserting that such a journey would involve traveling many miles through the lands of the Apaches. De Mézières then demanded that they at least follow him to Los Adaes. Again the chiefs refused. The Frenchman realized that they feared retribution for their previous acts of aggression. He therefore, decided to keep the many gifts that he had brought with him until the Wichitas agreed to his demands. The natives promised to gather again in the spring to consider the Spanish offer. They also vowed to remain peaceful and agreed to return the two brass cannon that had been taken from Diego de Parrilla in 1759.[13]

Although De Mézières was confident of the Wichitas' good intentions, most Spanish officials were skeptical. Some openly questioned De Mézières' talents and loyalty. Nevertheless, in 1771 he was rewarded with a treaty with the Wichitas. The tribe promised to refrain from further hostilities against Spaniards, to notify the commander of San Antonio should they approach that city, to punish their members who broke the treaty, to return the cannon, to return all Spanish captives, and to try to prevent future hostilities by the Comanches. Peace had been established at last along the Red River. For a time the Wichitas fulfilled the promises of the treaty, except the impossible one of controlling the Comanches.[14]

Athanase de Mézières's task was far from complete. English encroachment into the Red River valley to trade with the Wichitas and the continued obstinance of the Comanches required additional effort; however, he had accomplished the first phase of his plan to bring the natives of the Red River under the domination of Spain. He journeyed to the headwaters of the Brazos and Trinity rivers in 1772 and tried to persuade the natives there to accept Spanish rule peaceably.[15]

Soon after returning from Texas, De Mézières was granted permission to visit Europe to settle several personal matters. During his visit the king of Spain promoted him to lieutenant colonel and made him a knight of the Order of Saint Louis, in recognition of his accomplishments along the Red River.[16]

While De Mézières was in Europe, Indian problems erupted again in Texas. The Wichitas along the Red River, principally the Taovayas, had maintained their trade in horses with the English. The tribe secured horses by raiding Spanish settlements, as they had in earlier years. Also, the Osages who lived along the Arkansas River had begun intruding, agitating the natives and Europeans along the Red River. Because De

Mézières was not available, J. Gaignard, another Frenchman living in Louisiana, was appointed by Governor Unzaga y Amezaga to lead an expedition up the Red River to pacify the natives. Gaignard began his ascent of the Red River on October 1, 1773, at Natchitoches, accompanied by a small party of Spaniards and Frenchmen. The group moved up the Red River, passing through the lands of the Peticados to the Caddochos, where they stayed eighty-four days.[17]

On January 16, 1774, Gaignard left the Caddocho village, traveling with several Wichita guides. Soon after leaving, the Wichitas demanded that Gaignard give them booty. On February 5 the natives asked for blankets. In addition to doubts about the Wichitas, Gaignard also had serious doubts about the intentions of his companion, Manuel Sausier. These doubts were quickly confirmed. On February 10, Gaignard was approached by the chief of the Wichita village where he had camped; the headman informed him that Sausier had ordered the natives to seize half the goods that Gaignard had brought as gifts. The chief and his council refused to carry out the order, and the conniving Sausier was dismissed. Soon afterward the Wichitas attacked Gaignard and took all his goods. Gaignard reported, "They stole even my blanket; two days afterward snow fell and I nearly froze."[18]

Despite the loss of his goods Gaignard pushed on after obtaining new stores and arrived at a Wichita village one hundred leagues north of the Caddos. Gaignard found the Wichitas, whom he called Panis, separated into four principal groups along the Red River. He listed them as the Taovayas; Wichitas; or Quatchitas; Niscaniches; and Toyacanes; or Tawakonis. At the time of his visit Gaignard counted one thousand warriors. He asserted that the men did little but hunt and fight while the women were engaged in agriculture. To his disgust he noted that "when they take a slave capable of returning, they boil him and eat him" and that "they are very cruel, and are liars and thieves, the women as well as the

50

men."[19] He also found two cannon that had been taken from Colonel Parrilla.[20]

On February 22, a great assembly was held. A chief of the Wichitas spoke, declaring that he would love the Spaniards as he had the French and that he desired peace but wanted some small gift as a token of Spanish esteem. Gaignard complied with the chief's request by giving him eight pounds of powder, sixteen pounds of shot, twenty-four hunters' knives, and some tobacco. He then delivered a speech similar to that given by De Mézières in 1770, emphasizing that the French were gone forever and that the Spaniards were now allies. The Wichitas replied that they were entirely receptive to Spanish rule.[21]

Despite the Wichitas' protestations of loyalty to Spain, Gaignard learned two days after the meeting that the Indians were making plans for two groups to attack the Spaniards in Texas. Gaignard immediately demanded that the chief explain the reasons for the sudden change in attitude. He was told that many of the young men wished to make war because De Mézières's promises of gifts had not been fulfilled. Gaignard said that he would rectify the situation and asked the chief to stop the proposed raids. Gaignard then sent a messenger to Natchitoches to report what had happened. Despite his accomplishments thus far, Gaignard's troubles were only beginning.[22]

Gaignard's mission was to treat with both both the Wichitas and the Comanches. Although he was able to notify the leaders of one branch, the Naytane Comanches, of his wish to talk with them, subsequent events prevented the meeting. On March 4, 1774, one month after Gaignard notified the Comanches of his desire, a band of the Naytanes arrived at the Wichita village, returning from a battle with the Apaches. They reported that Spaniards in Texas had given firearms to another branch of the Comanches with whom the Naytanes were at that time unfriendly. This news created a great stir among the Wichitas, and they renewed their demand for gifts.

Gaignard was understandably discouraged by this turn of events. His hopes were revived a week later by the appearance of a chief of the Naytanes, who reported that the great chief of the Naytanes was pleased with Gaignard's presence, that the band desired peace, and that the great chief desired a meeting. Gaignard was hopeful that his mission finally would prove successful.[23]

Soon after the Naytanes left, a group of French traders arrived at the village from the Arkansas River. The Wichitas stated that they liked the French from the Arkansas better than those from Natchitoches because the former wanted horses, mules, and slaves—articles that were prohibited at Natchitoches.[24]

Gaignard remained at the Wichita village until October, 1774. Despite repeated requests by the Naytanes for Gaignard to visit their camp, he was unable to comply because of protests by the Wichitas, who steadily refused to allow the Frenchman to leave their village. Finally he decided to return to Natchitoches without completing his mission. The journey home was as unpleasant as his stay with the Wichitas had been. Nonetheless, Gaignard finally reached Natchitoches on November 24, 1774, a year after he had left.[25]

In his report Gaignard noted that further expeditions to the Wichitas and Comanches were mandatory. He emphasized that the trade from the Arkansas should be stopped and that only the most persuasive agents should be sent to deal with the natives on the Red. Spanish control of the Red River was critical. If the cord that bound the natives to Louisiana—the Red River—was severed, Spain would surrender domination of the vast area north of the Brazos River. The frontier still was restless—and in need of another expedition by De Mézières.[26]

By March, 1778, De Mézières was ready to focus his attention on the problems of the Red River frontier. With the blessing of Commandant General of the Interior Provinces

Teodoro de Croix, another Frenchman who had entered the service of Spain, De Mézières organized an expedition to visit the natives of the Red River. This mission was not to the Wichitas but rather to the natives who inhabited the headwaters of the Red River—the Comanches. The Wichitas had refrained from creating further disturbances in Texas. De Mézières's policy of liberal gift distribution seemingly had worked with that tribe. But the Comanches had remained a problem—stealing and raiding along a network of Spanish settlements in northern Texas and New Mexico. It was clear that neither missionization, which had been attempted until 1772, nor military conquest, which had been initiated after that date, could end the problems with the Comanches. Athanse de Mézières, therefore, was ordered again to utilize his extensive abilities in dealing with the natives.[27]

The expedition was organized at San Antonio de Béxar, present-day San Antonio, Texas. Accompanying De Mézières were a lieutenant and twenty-two soldiers from the garrison at Béxar, six militiamen whom he had brought from Natchitoches, and his own two sons. The party officially departed from San Antonio on March 18, 1778, following the Royal Road to Presidio Santa Cruz at Arroyo del Cíbolo.[28]

After adding thirteen militiamen and the missionary Francisco José de la Garga at Presidio Bucareli, the party arrived at the Cross Timbers near the Red River in early April. The Frenchman found Wichitas living in two villages, one on either side of the river. He estimated that the total number of natives there was more than eight hundred. He noted the advantages of the location: the river supplied potable water, the buffalo were numerous, and the Cross Timbers provided firewood. Despite these obvious advantages, De Mézières reported to De Croix that the Wichitas suffered from their neighbors—the Apaches on the south and the Osages on the north, who constantly attacked the Wichitas, and "the Comanche, who in the guise of friends, make them repeated vis-

its, always with the purpose of stealing."²⁹ He added that the
Wichitas pretended not to perceive the thefts of the Comanches "lest they should make other enemies, when they already have too many."³⁰

While he was with the Wichitas, De Mézières noted the advantages the Red River offered to Spaniards. He wrote, "Since
it joins the San Luis, or Micissipi [sic], sixty leagues above the
city of New Orleans, and five hundred below its source, taking
into consideration its sinuosity, we owe to it easy access to and
communication with the settlements of Natchitoches and the
neighboring Indian nations."³¹ He urged in his report to De
Croix that a settlement should be made among the Wichitas
on the Red, noting that it would aid in controlling the Comanches and that the location on the Red River would provide easy communication with the centers of government.³²

The Wichitas, who had treated Gaignard badly five years
before, greeted De Mézières with joy. They asked that Spaniards be sent to settle within their lands and noted that they
had refused admittance to two English traders from the Arkansas. De Mézières was pleased with the attitude of the
Wichitas because it reflected the success of his policies. He
also received the two brass cannon that had been taken from
Parrilla nearly twenty years earlier.³³

On April 8, 1778, De Mézières received a disturbing report.
Most of the warriors from a nearby Comanche village had recently ridden southward to attack Spaniards and had returned
with many horses and the scalp of the lieutenant paymaster of
Presidio San Antonio, whom they had found traveling across
the region. He also was informed that the Comanches had decided to cease their raids on San Antonio and the surrounding
area because the risks were too great and because the region
around Laredo provided an easier target. Greatly discouraged
by this report, De Mézières considered abandoning his mission. He wrote to De Croix: "Why should I go? To offer my
hand to hands that I might see stained in our blood? To be

54

witness of the spoliation of my nation? To fondle and protect barbarians whose crude understanding would ascribe our conduct to fear?"[34] After counseling with the chiefs of the Wichitas, however, De Mézières decided to continue.[35]

He dispatched a Comanche warrior, whom he had found wandering in the region, with a message to the Comanche chiefs, notifying them of his presence and demanding that they explain their recent actions. De Mézières included a warning that if the natives continued their warlike ways Spaniards would be forced to inflict punishment on their people. The Frenchman then waited at the village of the Wichitas, his spirits downcast and his expectations for success destroyed. Meanwhile he wrote to De Croix, suggesting that the Spaniards urge the various nations along the river to make war on the Comanches if the tribe refused to negotiate.[36]

De Mézières continued to wait at the village of the Wichitas during April. He then transferred his force southward to Bucareli, having received no replies to his message to the Comanches. The Comanches remained unsettled—as they would for many years to come.[37]

On May 2, 1778, De Mézières informed De Croix that his mission was completed and that he would return to his post at Natchitoches. De Croix and other officials in Mexico believed that De Mézières could better serve his country in Texas, and late in 1778 the Frenchman was ordered to return to Texas, where he would be promoted to colonel and given orders to lead another expedition to the frontier. When the aging Frenchman reached San Antonio in 1779, he learned that he had been appointed governor of Texas; however, he died on November 2 of that year before he could assume office.[38]

Despite the continued efforts by Commandant General De Croix and Domingo Cabello y Robles, who had been appointed governor of Texas after De Mézières's death, the Comanches remained a nuisance—and at times a major problem—for Spaniards in Texas and New Mexico. They had

been the great trouble in De Mézières's life, and they continued to haunt other officials who tried to deal with them.
Their enemies the Apaches, however, proved to be a more
pressing problem, and it was not until the fall of 1780 that a
new mission was sent to the Red River.[39]

Nicolas de la Matte, another Frenchman in the service of
Spain, was appointed to lead the expedition. La Matte set out
for the frontier in November, 1780, reaching the villages of
the Wichitas on the Red River three months later. He distributed gifts and harangued the natives to maintain peace.
He apparently did not reach the villages of the Comanches
but rather notified them through their nominal allies of the
Spanish desire for peace.[40]

Despite La Matte's efforts the Comanches continued to
sweep down from their villages on the Llano Estacado and the
Red River and spread death and destruction. In 1785 the citizens of Spanish Texas were relieved of the Comanche pressure by a treaty with the Kotsoteka and Penateka branches of
that tribe that temporarily established friendly relations. The
treaty was gained after Spanish officials in Texas decided to
overlook repeated depredations by the natives and after the
liberal distribution of gifts among the tribespeople. Indeed,
the eighth article of the treaty promised that "each year presents would be distributed to the chiefs and principal tribal
members as a proof and manifestation of our [the Spaniards]
good will."[41] Soon after the document was signed, the natives
began raiding into Texas, claiming that the Spaniards had not
fulfilled their portion of the agreement. Thus the treaty of
1785 was soon abrogated. From that time forward the Comanches continually raided Spanish settlements in Texas,
striking seemingly at will from the Gulf of Mexico to the Río
Grande. Spanish officials in Texas and in Mexico, at last acknowledging that they could not control the frontier, finally
abdicated authority in that region. They tried only to pacify
the natives with gifts and sporadically demanded that the

small presidial guard in Texas punish the troublemakers. The Comanches were a problem that another nation would have to settle—and only after great expenditures of money and men would a solution be achieved.[42]

While the Spaniards in Texas were unsuccessfully attempting to establish a permanent peace along their northern border, other problems pressed them for solution. Since the cession of Louisiana to Spain in 1762, Louisiana had been ruled by governors appointed by the viceroy in Cuba, while Texas and New Mexico had been under the control of the viceroy of New Spain, based in Mexico City. Although officials in each province had tried to cooperate with their counterparts in other provinces, communication had been sporadic and difficult. By 1780 officials in New Mexico realized that the provinces were in dire need of connecting roads. These roads would serve several purposes, in addition to making communication easier. They would allow supplies to be taken from Louisiana westward at far less expense than taking them overland from Mexico, and the products of Santa Fe could more easily be transported eastward. And the roads would bind the provinces together, an important advantage because the Spaniards feared encroachment from the newly established United States of America. For many years the French had been trading with the Wichitas on the Red River by crossing overland from the Arkansas. Spaniards thus hoped that roads connecting Santa Fe, San Antonio, and Natchitoches would discourage this trade, as well as intrusion by Americans.[43]

Regardless of the advantages that routes between Santa Fe, San Antonio, and Natchitoches would provide, Spaniards were still faced with the problem of surveying such roads. Less than a dozen expeditions had been made into the areas between these towns, and many of the men who had led the expeditions, such as De Mézières, were dead. Moreover, the country was inhabited by natives who often were hostile to Spaniards. The first problem was to find a man capable of blazing a trail between the cities, a man like St. Denis or De Mézières. Such a man was Pierre Vial, still another Frenchman who enlisted in the service in Spain.[44]

Pedro Vial, as he was known to the Spaniards of the Southwest, was born at Lyons, France, about the middle of the eighteenth century. Sometime during the 1770s he came to the New World, where he traded along the Missouri River during the American Revolution. Little is known of his background; however, he was in the Southwest in the 1780s, and he evidently had acquired much experience in the wilderness, to judge from his subsequent activities. The Red River would play an important role in the travels of Pedro Vial.[45]

The first matter at hand was the opening of a road from Santa Fe to San Antonio de Béxar. Because of Indian hostilities and insufficient knowledge of the region, travelers between the two cities were forced to follow a circuitous route: from Santa Fe southward to Chihuahua by way of El Paso, then to Saltillo, and from there to San Antonio—more than fifteen hundred miles. Finding a shorter route was Vial's first assignment.[46]

The origin of the order for a survey from Béxar to Santa Fe is obscure. It probably came from Jacobo Ugarte y Loyola, commandant general of the Interior Provinces, who was in a position to realize the importance of communication between the two cities. In any case, Governor Domingo Cabello of Texas was authorized to organize such an expedition. He also was informed that Pedro Vial, who had lived among the Indians of Texas for some time, had offered his services to fulfill this order. Undoubtedly pleasing to the economy-minded Spaniards was Vial's offer to make the trip with only one companion; the fewer travelers, the less money expended.[47]

Vial promised to blaze the most direct path possible from Béxar to Santa Fe, stopping at Indian villages along the way. On October 4, 1786, the intrepid explorer set out from San Antonio de Béxar; his only companion Cristóbal de los Santos. Because rivers were the only permanent and easily located

58

geographic markers in the area, the two followed the water-ways, reaching the Brazos in late October. They visited several villages of Wichitas during late October and December. From the last Wichita village that he visited, Vial sent out several warriors to survey the situation among the Comanches, through whose land the travelers had to pass. They returned with six Comanches, who invited Vial to visit their village. It was there that the Frenchman met Guaquangas (Coat of Mail), who wanted the Europeans to accompany him to San Antonio. Vial refused, stating that he would continue his journey. After leaving the Comanches on January 18, the two wintered in an arroyo near present-day Burkburnett, Texas, until March 4, 1787.[48]

On March 15, Vial reached the destination he had been seeking since leaving San Antonio—the Red River. Evidently he had learned previously that the Red would guide him to Santa Fe, for his route from San Antonio had been generally north. Certainly Vial knew that his march toward his destination was not a direct one, and he was simply seeking a signpost—the Red River. During his journey from San Antonio to the Red he demonstrated his propensity for using streams as natural means of navigation by following the Colorado and the Brazos.[49]

After he reached the Red River, Vial followed the stream westward. Sometime during this portion of the journey Vial and Santos were joined by the Comanche chief Zoquine, who promised to guide them to Santa Fe. Despite the presence of the chief, the party was threatened by another group of Comanches, who asserted that Vial had come to take the natives to Santa Fe, where they would be murdered. Vial responded with his usual confidence that these men were liars and that the Spaniards were not blackhearted like the Comanches. His strong statement served him well, and the natives allowed him to continue.[50]

The explorer followed the Red through most of April, leaving the stream where it entered the Llano Estacado. From the

Red, Vial went to the South Canadian, which he followed into New Mexico. On May 26, 1787, he reported to Spanish officials at Santa Fe, having journeyed by way of north Texas from the city of Saint Anthony to the city of the Holy Faith for the first time. He and Santos had traveled more than one thousand miles, most of them alone, in less than one year. Moreover, they had passed through the lands of the most-feared Indians in the Southwest. This was the first of Vial's remarkable accomplishments.[51]

Pedro Vial's journey from San Antonio to Santa Fe was a great feat of exploration and courage; however, he found Spanish officials in New Mexico unsatisfied. There must be another, more direct route between the two cities. In his effort to use the Red River as a guide, Vial had made his road too circuitous, too time-consuming, and too dangerous. They determined to send another explorer to find a more direct connection. Juan Bautista de Anza, the governor of New Mexico, himself an accomplished explorer, appointed José Mares to lead another expedition. Mares was ordered to travel from Santa Fe to San Antonio by the most direct route possible. On July 31, 1787, less than two months after Vial reached Santa Fe, Mares departed for San Antonio. He was accompanied by Cristóbal de los Santos, Pedro Vial's former companion, and Alejandro Martín, an Indian interpreter who had worked for officials in New Mexico.[52]

San Antonio was more than five hundred miles east and south of Santa Fe, at a forty-five-degree angle from the city. Mares's direction should have been southeast to open the most direct route between the two outposts. He began his journey in that direction, traveling to the Pecos and then to the Gallianas; however, he then turned northeast, heading for the Red River. He ascended the Llano Estacado and reached the Tule River, a tributary of the Red. Leaving the Tule on the Llano, Mares marched to the Pease River, another tributary of the Red, followed the Pease for several days, and then marched to the Wichita River. He crossed that stream and continued to the Little Wichita, which he called Río de los Taguayazes, or River of the Taovayas (for the subtribe of the Wichitas who lived near the mouth of the stream, on the Red River). Throughout this portion of the journey the Spaniard repeatedly met bands of Comanches, who greeted him as a friend and traveled with him for varying lengths of time. Many of the natives accompanied him to the village of the Wichitas to trade.

On September 5, 1787, Mares reached the villages on the Red, where he and his party were greeted as friends by the natives. The Spaniards stayed four days on the Red River, leaving on September 9. From the Red, Mares led his expedition almost directly toward San Antonio, forming a rough right angle. Why had the Spaniard, after receiving strict orders to find the most direct route, chosen to repeat Vial's visit to the Red? Mares's return journey to Santa Fe—after severe chastisement by the governor of Texas for going by way of the Red—was one-third shorter than his march from Santa Fe to San Antonio. Undoubtedly Mares went to the Red River for two similar reasons: the Wichita villages on the river had become well-known points, after their discovery by De Mézières and Vial, and the river, too, was well known. By going to the Red River, Mares split his journey to San Antonio into two portions, blazing a new trail only in the first part. His second reason was that because the Wichita villages were well known and trading centers for natives in the region a route from Santa Fe to San Antonio should pass through that important marketplace.[53]

José Mares returned to Santa Fe in 1788, making the journey in four months. His trip pleased Spanish officials in New Mexico because it demonstrated the possibility of direct traffic between the major cities of New Mexico and Texas. The third city of the Spanish trinity in the Interior Provinces, Natchitoches, remained separated from the others. It was perhaps the most important of the three because of its location on the navigable Red River. That made it an important link in any

61

future trading system the Spaniards might devise. If Santa Fe and San Antonio were joined to Natchitoches by good roads, supplies could be brought to the post on the Red by water and from there transferred to the other posts by road. Products from New Mexico and Texas could be shipped out of the interior by the same route. Obviously the Spaniards' next step was to connect Natchitoches with its sister outposts.[54]

Before Mares left San Antonio, Vial had suggested to Governor Anza an expedition from Santa Fe to Natchitoches. The governor had forwarded Vial's comments to Commandant General Jacobo Ugarte. Evidently Vial believed that his work between San Antonio and Santa Fe had been sufficient and did not wish to seek a more direct route. Despite their dissatisfaction with Vial's first expedition, Spanish officials were willing to utilize his experience and courage once again to open a road from Santa Fe to Natchitoches. Anza's replacement as governor of New Mexico, Fernando de la Concha, accepted Vial's offer to go to Louisiana, and on June 24, 1788, less than a month after Mares returned from San Antonio, Pedro Vial set out once more into the wilderness. With Vial went four Spaniards who would make the entire journey with him. Several others would make only part of the trip, including Santiago Fernández, who would go only as far as the Wichita villages on the Red River and return to Santa Fe to report the progress of the mission to the Spanish officials. The four who would accompany Vial were Francisco Xavier Fragoso, José María Romero, Gregorio Leyva, and Juan Lucero.[55]

The expedition set out in the same direction that Mares had taken a year before, crossing the Pecos and Gallinas rivers to the headwaters of the Red River and passing the region near present-day Tucumcari, New Mexico. Near Palo Duro Canyon, Vial and the others reached the Prairie Dog Town Fork of the Red River, which they followed eastward. While they followed the river, which the Spaniards called Río Blanco, they were met by a Comanche near the mouth of Tule

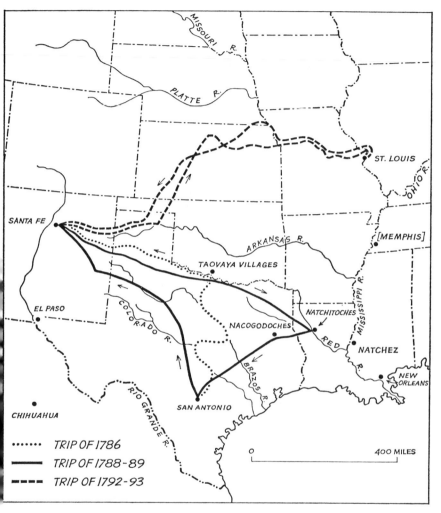

The routes of Pedro Vial's three principal trips to Santa Fe. From *Pedro Vial and the Roads to Santa Fe*, by Noel M. Loomis and Abraham P. Nasatir.

River. He took the Spaniards to his camp, where they were treated as guests and refreshed from their journey. After visiting with the Comanches, the group set out eastward again, following the river. About the middle of July the group descended from the Llano and continued along the stream, noting the entrance of the North Fork and the Pease rivers, which greatly enlarged the Red's size. Near the mouths of these streams several groups of Comanches were sighted. They, like the ones met earlier, were friendly to the Spaniards and volunteered to guide the party to the villages of the Wichitas. Vial accepted the offer because among them were those who had led him to Santa Fe on his first exploration.[56]

On July 20, Vial reached the mouths of the Wichita River and Cache Creek, which entered the Red from the south and north, respectively. The next day the party found the Wichita camps that Vial had visited a year and a half before and that Mares had passed through earlier. The villages had changed little from the time when De Mézières had visited them in 1778, although the population of both appeared to have decreased markedly. De Mézières reported the number of inhabitants as more than eight hundred, but Vial found each village containing only seventeen huts. Vial's chronicler, Francisco Fragoso, noted a third village east of the two that had not been reported earlier. Possibly the presence of this third village accounted for the decrease in the population of the other two settlements.[57]

The Spaniards spent six days with the Wichitas. The stop allowed them and their animals to prepare for the last portion of the journey to Natchitoches. On May 26 they set out from the last Wichita village, leaving the Red River to continue their travel overland. Evidently Vial knew that by cutting across present-day east Texas he could reach Natchitoches much quicker than by following the river along the Great Bend. The party marched almost directly to Natchitoches, crossing the headwaters of the Trinity north of present-day

Dallas. During this portion of the march Fragoso was repeat-edly impressed by the terrain, noting the Cross Timbers and the divide between the watersheds of the Red and Trinity rivers where two small streams rose, one flowing north, the other south. On August 14 they crossed the Sabine, reaching settled areas near the abandoned site of Los Adaes. Six days later the group entered Natchitoches, ending a journey of more than nine hundred miles.[58]

Pedro Vial stayed at Natchitoches for two weeks and then set out for San Antonio. After a stop in San Antonio he trav-eled to Santa Fe, which he reached on August 20, 1789. In less than three years he had completed the original task that had been given him by officials of the Interior Provinces—with a little help from Mares. From October 4, 1786, to Au-gust 20, 1789, he had crosed the entire breadth of Texas once, joining Santa Fe, San Antonio, and Natchitoches. Through-out his travels the Red River had played a major role, guiding him from San Antonio to Santa Fe, as it had Mares. Like an aquatic Polaris, the Red was a sign that pointed the way for Pedro Vial.[59]

Despite the successes of Vial and Mares in connecting Santa Fe, San Antonio, and Natchitoches, the roads did not prevent the encroachment of foreigners into Spanish terri-tory. A decade after Vial's journey from Santa Fe to Natchi-toches, Louisiana's fate again was decided by European di-plomacy: by the Treaty of San Ildefonso the province was retroceded to France by Spain. Napoleon had decided to re-build the French empire in North America.

5.

Spain's New Foe

France had lost Louisiana in 1762 because of problems not connected with the province. In 1803 the situation recurred. Because his armies could not quell the insurrection in Santo Domingo, because war was imminent in Europe, and because he did not want Louisiana to fall into the hands of the British, Napolean, having regained Louisiana, sold the province to willing Americans for the bargain price of fifteen million dollars. Despite Thomas Jefferson's constitutional objections to the purchase, the United States quickly accepted the province of Louisiana as its own. The only question was, What, exactly, had the United States bought? The French refused to define what they had sold, answering American questions concerning the boundaries of Louisiana with suggestions that obscure borders provided a chance to steal some Spanish land. The Spaniards, who remained in physical control of the province until its transfer to the United States, had an answer, but the United States was unwilling to accept their somewhat biased judgment. The only boundary of any certainty was the Mississippi. West of that great stream the continent remained virginal and unexplored except for the small areas of Spanish occupation in the Southwest. There were serious questions concerning the validity of Spanish claims, especially along the Red River.

For many years Jefferson had been interested in the exploration of the trans-Mississippi West, suggesting various missions during the latter part of the eighteenth century. As president his interest had not waned. He suggested the expedition of Meriwether Lewis and William Clark before the Louisiana Purchase was made and became American soil by an accident of European diplomacy. Moreover, Jefferson's interest was not limited to the Northwest. In 1803 the president wrote to three individuals asking for information regarding the Red River: Daniel Clark, the American consul at New Orleans; William Dunbar, the foremost scientist of the Mississippi Valley; and William C. C. Claiborne, governor of the newly created Louisiana Territory. The responses to Jefferson's questions were vague, general, and brief. He therefore determined, that another expedition, similar to that of Lewis and Clark, was in order. He wrote William Dunbar requesting him to lead an expedition up the Red River to its source and to cross over to the Arkansas and descend that stream. He noted that his plans were contingent on the appropriation of funds by Congress. Happily the legislative branch was cooperative, and three thousand dollars were set aside for the suggested purpose—exploration of the Red and Arkansas rivers. Jefferson wrote Dunbar again, asking him to make preparations for the journey. He also informed Dunbar that George Hunter, a chemist living in Philadelphia, would accompany the mission to make scientific observations.[1]

As he prepared for the proposed journey up the Red, Dunbar wrote to Peter Walker, a trader who frequently ascended the river, repeating the questions about the stream that Jefferson had asked earlier. He made few physical preparations, however. When Hunter arrived at Dunbar's plantation on the Mississippi, after descending the Ohio and Mississippi rivers by flatboat, he learned that boats and provisions for the journey had not yet been acquired. Lieutenant Colonel Constant Freeman, military commander at New Orleans, had been ordered by Secretary of War Henry Dearborn to provide these articles, but he had decided to wait until Hunter's arrival to begin preparations. Thus the expedition was behind schedule before setting out.[2]

67

Hunter went on to New Orleans. There he altered the flat-boat in which he had descended the Mississippi and obtained the provisions for the journey. After two months in New Orleans, Hunter returned to Dunbar's plantation, where he learned that the expedition had again been delayed. In July, President Jefferson had been visited by a delegation of Osages who informed him of a split in their nation. It had resulted in the settlement of one band on the Verdigris River, a tributary of the Arkansas in present-day Oklahoma, and one band on the Neosho River, another tributary of the Arkansas, east of the Verdigris. They warned Jefferson that an American expedition on the Arkansas would be attacked by the band on the Verdigris. Therefore Jefferson had written Dunbar to suggest postponement of the proposed expedition to the Red and Arkansas. Instead Dunbar and Hunter were to ascend the Ouachita (pronounced "Wash'i-tah"), a tributary of the Red flowing from south-central Arkansas. They were to enter the Red in central Louisiana, in order to utilize the men and supplies that had been collected. The president urged Dunbar to forward a report of his actions so that Congress could be apprised of the journey—and asked to appropriate additional funds. Finally, Jefferson noted that the delay was fortunate because it would allow Americans to settle difficulties that had arisen with the Spaniards over the Texas-Louisiana boundary.[3]

Spain and the United States had quarreled because of the vagueness of the limits of Louisiana. France, the conduit through which Louisiana had passed to the United States, had asserted that the province included Texas, citing La Salle's settlement as proof of the claim. Spanish officials proclaimed that the Arkansas was the southern boundary of Louisiana, arguing that the province of Texas had expanded during the years of Spanish domination in Louisiana (1762–1800). Therefore they were not willing to allow an American exploring party to ascend the Red River. Their attitude had been summarized in Commandant General Nemesio Salcedo's proclamation by May, 1804, that all American attempts to enter Texas or to survey the boundaries of Louisiana would be stopped and the men arrested. Dunbar and Hunter wisely decided that the Ouachita would make an acceptable object of exploration—no Spaniards were there.[4]

The expedition left the Mississippi on October 4, 1804, and returned in February, 1805, after reaching the head of navigation on the Ouachita near the mouth of the Fourche de Chalfat. Although the first American expedition on the Red River proved abortive, the mission was not entirely unsuccessful. The reports by Hunter and Dunbar contained valuable advice for later explorers in the area: special boats were needed, an authoritative officer was mandatory to control the enlisted men, and sophisticated scientific equipment was necessary for making workable observations.[5]

While Hunter and Dunbar had been waiting to ascend the Ouachita, President Jefferson was approached by a man with additional information concerning the Red River. John C. Sibley, a native of Massachusetts, had settled in Natchitoches in 1802 and had involved himself in the affairs of the area. More important to Jefferson, Sibley had journeyed up the Red River in 1803, making copious notes and observations. In March, 1804, he wrote to Jefferson relating his geographic knowledge of the region and of its natives. It was limited to the lower reaches of the river below the Great Bend, but his letters whetted Jefferson's appetite—and got Sibley an appointment as contrast surgeon for the Natchitoches area. In 1805, Jefferson appointed Sibley to head the Natchitoches Indian Factory, which burdened him with the task of controlling the natives of the Louisiana-Texas frontier. He performed the job well, remaining a thorn in the side of the Spaniards, as had St. Denis a hundred years earlier.[6]

Jefferson was intent on sending an expedition up the Red River despite the failure of Hunter and Dunbar to do so. Ironically, the president's interest was inspired by love of scientific knowledge rather than a lust for geographic information that would aid in the dispute with Spain. It made little difference to the scholarly chief executive that the Red River would soon become a major portion of his nation's boundary and that the course of the river would create dissension for more than a century. Spanish officials, however, were highly interested in the political implications of an American mission and were determined to prevent such an occurrence.

The president had two problems: he needed someone to lead the expedition, and he needed some means of obtaining Spanish cooperation, or, at least, Spanish permission for the expedition.[7] Neither Dunbar nor Hunter was willing to assume leadership of the new mission. Thomas Freeman was selected to lead the exploration, but Jefferson realized that Freeman, an experienced surveyor, could not perform the necessary botanical observations. Therefore, Peter Custis was selected to accompany the party as the scientific specialist. Jefferson, meanwhile, had decided that the party should limit its exploration to the Red River, rather than ascending the Red and marching overland to the source of the Arkansas. Restricting the exploration to the Red would avoid the problems of transporting the men and their supplies overland and the difficulties with the Osages on the Arkansas.

After securing a leader for the mission, Jefferson's second problem—the Spaniards—proved more difficult.[8] In a letter to Dunbar that spoke of new goals for the expedition, Jefferson asked him to write to Governor Claiborne of Louisiana. Dunbar was to ask Claiborne to approach the former governor of Spanish Louisiana, the Marqués de Casa Calvo, who had remained in New Orleans as a boundary commissioner, to ask for a passport for the expedition. Claiborne was dutifully informed, and in July, 1805, he asked Casa Calvo for the desired document. The American was careful to emphasize that the mission was solely for purpose of gathering scientific data and was in no way an encroachment on Spanish territory. Despite these promises Casa Calvo was leery of the United States. He was certain that the mission was designed to collect military information about the region and to agitate the natives against the Spaniards. The Marqués also was confident that the Americans were planning a military invasion of the region to secure their claims. But Claiborne's request was difficult to refuse. In addition to vows of good faith the Americans offered to allow Spaniards to accompany the mission, and the request was endorsed by Secretary Andrés López Armesto of the Spanish boundary commission. Casa Calvo decided to grant his permission while simultaneously informing Spanish officials in Texas of the planned mission. He noted that he could not interfere with any decisions made in Texas concerning the expedition. That effectively negated the power of the passport given to Claiborne. What value has a passport that carries no authority? Casa Calvo had determined to remain friendly to the Americans, while assuring that the Spanish officials in Texas would act against the proposed mission. Thus he avoided making a decision.[9]

Casa Calvo's actions stirred both Americans and Spaniards to action. Commandant General Salcedo, who had earlier issued an order banning all Americans from Texas, moved to preclude any advance into Spanish territory by ordering troops to be garrisoned at Bayou Pierre (near the site of the early post of Los Adaes). They would block the path of the proposed expedition. In February, 1806, the commander of the American detachment at Natchitoches sent a force of sixty men to compel the Spaniards to withdraw. This force, commanded by Captain Edward Turner, found the Spanish force of twenty men near Los Adaes. The Spanish officer in charge, Ensign José María Gonzáles, protested but agreed to withdraw. Although the action cleared the path for the expedition, it strengthened the Spanish distrust of Americans. In addition, the Marqués de Casa Calvo was asked to remove himself from United States soil on February 12, 1806. This action further increased the suspicions of Spaniards toward the Americans and decreased the value of the passport that Casa Calvo had given Claiborne.[10]

Despite all these problems the expedition departed in

April, 1806, almost a year after Jefferson had suggested it. The leaders of the party were Freeman and Custis; Lieutenant Enoch Humphrey, assistant to Custis in making botanical observations; and Captain Richard Sparks, the military commander of the group. Two noncommissioned officers and seventeen privates were added to the company, increasing the number in the expedition to thirty-seven.[11]

Late in May the party left Natchitoches. Above that village the river became increasingly difficult to navigate because of driftwood and mud that clogged the channel. It was the lower part of the "Great Raft" that lay farther north. Jams in the river were called rafts because they bore a resemblance to rafts that had been formed by sticking logs and brush together with mud. The rafts made travel tortuous and slow. Boats had to be lifted over shallows created by collections of wood and mud, and a serpentine course was followed because the rafts had filled the main bed of the river, leaving the waters to flow through myriad miniature channels. Much time was wasted searching for open paths through the woody barrier because channels were continually changing—opening and closing. A course that was open one day might be closed the next by the whims of water and wood.

On June 8 the party's problems increased. A runner from John Sibley at Natchitoches notified Freeman that a Spanish force of considerable magnitude had left Nacogdoches, the center of Spanish authority in east Texas, with orders to stop the Americans. That afternoon Sibley reached the party with the same warning. Although Freeman had no wish to fight a larger Spanish force, he and his fellow explorers decided to push on with hopes of evading the Spaniards.

On June 11 the party reached the Great Raft, an almost solid mass of wood, brush, and mud that had been jammed together by wind and water to clog the river's channel for more than fifty miles. Attempting to pass through the obstacle was useless. Therefore the party, led by French guides, followed a circuitous path around the jam that consumed more than one hundred miles. Two hundred miles above Natchitoches and just below the Great Bend of the Red, the group reentered the unclogged channel of the river. Two days after they had passed the raft, the explorers reached the village of the Alabama-Coushatta Indians. This tribe had moved into the region from the east during the latter part of the eighteenth century, fleeing from the pressures of white men. The natives received the explorers well. At the village Freeman received news that a Spanish force of approximately three hundred had recently visited a nearby Caddo village searching for the Americans.

In keeping with the American policy of courting the friendship of Indians in that area, Freeman gave the chief presents, including an American flag. On July 1 chiefs from the neighboring Caddo villages arrived, and Freeman again distributed gifts. He made speeches declaring that Americans were friends of the natives and praising the chiefs for their abilities and bravery. The Indians replied by lauding the Americans, promising never to make war on whites, and inviting them to visit their villages often. Thus the Americans followed the French policy of endearing themselves to the natives of the region. Two days after their arrival the Caddos departed, promising to warn the Americans of movements by the Spaniards.

After winning the friendship of the natives, the party left the Alabama-Coushatta village on July 11 and continued upriver to enter the Great Bend. The explorers emerged from the bend two weeks after leaving the village and reached the location of the Nassonite village where La Harpe had erected his trading post eighty-seven years earlier. A few rotting posts were the only remains of the old French fort. The day after the explorers arrived at the abandoned fort, they were met by three Caddo Indians, who warned that the Spaniards had recently visited their villages. The Spanish commander, whose force numbered one thousand, had berated the chiefs for accepting the Americans. He had pulled down the flag that Freeman had left and had sworn to kill the American ex-

73

plorers if they attempted to continue their journey. The natives were evidently impressed by this show of Spanish strength
and urged the Americans to retreat and avoid contact with
the terrible Spaniards. Thomas Freeman, however, rejected
their admonitions and commanded his force to push onward.

Despite his determination to continue, Freeman realized
that the Spanish force presented a serious threat to his party
and his mission. Therefore he ordered his men to bury part of
their equipment, including their instruments and notes. He
also warned them to remain alert. The group then advanced
cautiously, expecting to meet Spaniards at each turn of the
river.

While the American force had been visiting with the natives and pushing upriver, the Spaniards in Texas had been
busy. After the Spanish force had been ejected from the area
around Bayou Pierre by the Americans under Turner, Spanish
officials in Texas had believed that armed conflict along the
Red River was imminent. The commander of the forces at
Nacogdoches, Captain Sebastian Rodríguez, had asked that
his garrison be increased and that he be replaced by a more
experienced officer. Governor Antonio Cordero y Bustamante
evidently had agreed with Rodríguez because Captain Francisco Viana had been placed in command at Nacogdoches in
June. Viana had wasted little time in preparing for the expected American assault. He had bolstered garrisons in east
Texas and had decided to repulse the American expedition as
it traveled up the Red River. On July 12 he left Nacogdoches
for the river. Moving quickly and forcefully, the Spaniards
reached the villages of the Caddos, where they learned of the
recent visit by Americans. Realizing that they would follow
the river's circuitous route, Viana marched overland, arriving
at the river ahead of the Americans. He arranged his force on
the river and readied them for battle, expecting armed conflict with the approaching Americans.[12]

On July 28 the Americans reached the waiting Spaniards,
but the expected battle did not occur. Instead the American

and Spanish officers met to find a peaceful solution to the impasse. Viana demanded that the Americans withdraw, promising to enforce his demand with arms if necessary. Freeman had little choice. Either he could retreat or his party would perish. The American demanded that Viana put his reasons for turning back the expedition in writing. He evidently wished to have some document to give President Jefferson when he returned without completing the mission. Viana stubbornly refused, stating only that he was acting in accord with the wishes of officials in Mexico. The Spaniard, confident in his numerical superiority, ended the meeting by asking when the Americans planned to depart. The next day the Americans withdrew, leaving the Spaniards victorious, although many of Freeman's party had favored battle.[13]

In August, Freeman's party returned to Natchitoches, having overcome the elements and the river but not the Spaniards. Again President Jefferson's hopes of exploring the Red River had been dashed by the forces of international diplomacy and Spanish arms. The results of Freeman's mission were not entirely negative, however. The Americans had succeeded in winning the friendship of the Alabama-Coushattas and the Caddos. Viana's unseemly behavior at the village of the Caddos had demonstrated to the natives the differences in attitude of Spaniards and Americans. Thus, while Viana had won an immediate victory for his nation, he had helped lay the foundation for permanent American control of the region along the Red.[14]

Repulsion of the American exploring party was seen by Spanish officials in Texas as a prelude to full-scale conflict along the border. The Spaniards believed that the expedition had been arranged to collect military information and to win the aid of the natives of northeastern Texas. Therefore, they believed, the Americans, thwarted in their exploring, would soon return in force to seize the region west of the Red River. Preparations to meet such an invasion had already been started before Freeman was turned back. Viana's appointment had been part of the strengthening of the defenses of east Texas, as had been the transferring of troops from Mexico to Texas. Furthermore, Lieutenant Colonel Simón de Herrera, the governor of Nueva Santander, had been ordered by Commandant General Salcedo to take military control of east Texas. By the time Viana was sending Thomas Freeman back down the Red River, there were more than thirteen hundred Spanish troops in Texas, more than eight hundred of them garrisoned at Nacogdoches. Spanish troops were also stationed east of the Sabine River near the site of Los Adaes. About four hundred men of the garrison at Nacogdoches were sent to Bayou Pierre under the command of Colonel Herrera. The Spaniards were determined to defend their territory east of the Sabine along the Red.[15]

In Louisiana the Americans were equally determined to drive the Spaniards west of the Sabine. The Spaniards were seen as counterrevolutionaries who were the enemies of United States republicanism. Too, many Americans coveted the rich lands that lay between the Red and Sabine rivers. Feeling for war ran high in Louisiana; orators called for militiamen to rally together to aid the army in driving back the Spanish invaders. Newspapers proclaimed that the American Revolution should be spread to the people of Texas. Finally, General James Wilkinson, the military commander of Louisiana, moved toward the Texas-Louisiana border accompanied by reinforcements for the garrison at Natchitoches.[16]

On reaching Natchitoches, Wilkinson notified Governor Cordero y Bustamante that the Spanish force at Bayou Pierre had to be removed or conflict would result. Cordero replied that his authority did not include yielding Spanish territory to foreign armies. It was September, and war seemed inevitable.[17]

James Wilkinson did not want war. His allegedly treasonable association with Aaron Burr was reaching a climax, and the general opposed any conflict with the Spaniards that would draw attention to his district. His orders, however, were explicit: the Spanish force east of the Sabine had to be ejected. Wilkinson had little choice but to initiate action if the Spaniards would not retreat.[18]

Suddenly, almost as if by design, Herrera moved west of the Sabine. Inexplicably the Spaniard had ordered his force away from Bayou Pierre. Possibly Herrera had decided that his position was untenable; possibly he had decided that the starvation and illness plaguing his troops had to be eased. Whatever his motive, Herrera's move ended the crisis. His only comment to his superiors was that he was preserving the territory of his nation. Possibly he believed that by avoiding a military defeat Spain might regain the area by diplomacy.[19]

Wilkinson, who was about to betray Aaron Burr, was astounded by Herrera's move but was not stumped for a course of action. Four weeks after the Spaniards withdrew, Wilkinson moved to the Sabine. There he issued a proposal to the Spanish officials: If Spaniards would remain west of the Sabine, Americans would remain east of the Arroyo Hondo; the area in between would become neutral ground separating the two nations. On November 4, 1806, Herrera agreed—without consulting his superiors. Despite Herreras oversight, officials in Mexico City subsequently gave their consent to the agreement, realizing that this pragmatic solution was better than a military defeat. The permanent settlement of the disputed border between Louisiana and Texas would be left to diplomats in Washington and Madrid. Once more the Red River was the boundary between Texas and Louisiana.[20]

While these pawns were jousting along the frontier, diplomats were making little progress in Europe. Although a commission had been established after the Louisiana Purchase to define the borders of Louisiana and Texas, and although James Monroe and Charles Cotesworth Pinckney had been sent to Spain, no settlement had been reached. The international impasse was similar to the one that Wilkinson and Herrera had solved. Carlos IV, the king of Spain, and his prime minister, Manuel de Godoy, the self-styled Prince of the Peace, were determined to hold Florida and Texas. The Americans were hopeful of gaining at least part of these provinces. Along the border between Texas and Louisiana, Americans were willing to compromise: the Colorado River instead of the Río Grande was an acceptable boundary for Texas. This solution would have split the province of Texas in half, giving the Americans the rich, fertile portion and leaving the Spaniards the barren, wild area. But Spain remained adamant—and its position was supported by Napoleon and the armies of France. Therefore war was not a solution that the United States considered after Napoleon's intentions were made clear to General John Armstrong, the American minister in France. Unfortunately, the diplomats could not arrange a temporary settlement as the soldiers had on the frontier. Soon Europe was aflame with war, and Texas had to wait. [21]

The world war that Napoleon created—and almost won—ended in 1815. Nothing was the same again after the great dictator retired into exile. Spain had lost—or was losing—much of its empire in America, and the new king, Ferdinand VII, was ill-prepared to guide his nation back to supremacy. The United States emerged from the war scarred and in debt; Americans, however, reacted boldly and adventurously. The young nation, on the verge of defeat in 1814, convinced itself in 1815 that Andrew Jackson's victory at New Orleans had recouped all previous losses and that the United States was entering a golden era of republicanism while Europe was sinking into a leaden period of decadence. [22]

European leaders seemed bent on fulfilling American prophecies. In Vienna representatives from France, Austria, and Prussia worked to reap the spoils of war rather than raise the world from the shambles that Napoleon had made. Spain demanded that the Congress of Vienna return Louisiana, or at least give it the fifteen million dollars that France had received for the province. The Congress refused, realizing that Spain would have to accept the decisions it made. England watched uneasily as it grew more and more isolated from its European neighbors. [23]

78

Spain's problems were legion. Revolutions had swept its American colonies; Mexico, long a money-making province, was in the midst of revolt; and colonies throughout South America were burning with rebellion. Spanish officials were hard pressed in Europe, as well as in America, yet had to settle the boundaries of the Louisiana Purchase—and time had not strengthened their position.[24]

The task of negotiating a settlement fell to the Spanish minister to the United States, Luis de Onís y Gonzáles, a career diplomat whose uncle had been the Spanish ambassador to Saxony and Russia. Onís had been the minister to Saxony and had been in charge of relations with France before his appointment to Washington in October, 1809.[25]

Onís's arrival in the United States had not been greeted with enthusiasm. Indeed, President James Madison had refused to recognize the Spaniard's appointment because of the civil war in Spain. Onís had chafed under this lack of recognition and had made his feelings known to all concerned. By 1814 Onís was extremely unpopular with American officials, including Secretary of State James Monroe, who wrote the American minister in Madrid, George Erving, that Onís was unwelcome in Washington and that the administration would favor his replacement. Because the Spanish government was insistent that Onís remain in the United States, however, American officials soon warmed to the diplomat.[26]

Meanwhile, the Americans had been attempting to settle the problem by diplomacy in Madrid. In 1815, Erving was sent to Madrid to consult with the Spanish secretary of state for foreign affairs, Pedro Cevallos. The Spaniards were not willing to discuss the matter, much to Secretary Monroe's disgust. In August, 1816, Cevallos refused to speak with Erving, asserting that all papers concerning the problem had been sent to Onís. Thus negotiations were transferred to Washington at the insistence of the Spanish government. Indeed, Spaniards had transferred the talks without consulting the Americans or even notifying them.[27]

With the removal of the talks to Washington, the situation surrounding the problem of defining the Louisiana Purchase began to improve. Pedro Cevallos, who had repeatedly demonstrated his inadequacy as a diplomat, was replaced by José García de León y Pizarro, a talented and perceptive diplomat who possessed both the ability and the temperament to aid in the solution of the problem. Under his leadership and guidance, Onís could negotiate freely and seriously. The tightly reined administration of Cevallos had prevented such movements.[28]

The appointment in 1817 of John Quincy Adams as secretary of state in Monroe's administration aided greatly in creating circumstances favorable to a settlement of the dispute between Spain and the United States. Adams had spent most of his life in the diplomatic service. In 1781, while a teenager, he had gone to the Russian court as secretary to the American minister, Charles Francis Dana. He had later served as American consul to Prussia and Russia, and he had been an important member of the American committee negotiating at Ghent during the talks that ended the War of 1812. Long before 1817 he had deserted the Federalism of his father in favor of Jefferson's Republicanism. Therefore, in light of his diplomatic experience and his political inclination, he was a natural choice to head the Department of State.[29]

Perhaps the most important attribute that Adams carried to the Department of State was the scope and depth of his knowledge. Having visited many of the nations of Europe and learned the nature of many of the people of the world, Adams was well qualified to treat with the Spanish minister on any problem, including the settlement of the boundary between the United States and the Spanish colonies in the New World.[30]

Although Onís had been given full power to settle the problem in 1816, several factors delayed initiating negotiations. Pizarro's administration in Spain needed time to de-

John Quincy Adams. As Secretary of State in James Monroe's administration he negotiated the treaty of 1819 with Spanish minister Don Lois Onís, making the Red River a substantial part of the western boundary of the United States. Courtesy of the National Archives.

velop its policies, and the formation of Monroe's administration after the election of 1816 delayed matters until the spring of 1817. At the end of the summer of that year Onís was provided with a full set of instructions, similar to those Spain had already presented: the province of Louisiana had limited and well-defined borders that did not include Texas or west Florida. The Spaniards also suggested that the Floridas might be sold to Great Britain.[31]

Onís had little confidence in the instructions that his government had forwarded. The United States was in no mood to forsake its claims, and there was movement afoot in Congress, led by a young westerner named Henry Clay, to recognize the independence of Spain's rebellious colonies in South America. With apprehension Onís arranged a meeting with Secretary Adams on December 1, 1817, to announce his nation's proposals. As expected, Onís's demands were rejected immediately by Adams. Then the two diplomats began detailed talks, discussing the respective needs of their nations. These negotiations would last many days and search into many subjects before a final agreement was reached.[32]

Despite Adams's rejection of his offers, Onís evidently believed that he and the New Englander could hammer out an agreement. He was eager for a conclusion to the negotiations because he feared overt American aggression. His nervous state was further aggravated by Great Britain's offer to mediate the dispute in December, 1817. Should the Americans learn of the English interest in the affair, they might be spurred to military action. Onís did not mention the matter to Adams and urged his superiors to move the talks back to Madrid, where the delays in communication could be avoided.[33]

In January 1818, Adams and Onís again met to discuss their differences. Adams chided the Spaniard for wasting time, but Onís replied that any treaty made quickly would have to be based on *uti possidetis* as of 1809; each nation would receive the territory it had possessed that year. This arrangement was clearly unacceptable to the United States because it would be deprived of Texas and most of Florida. Thus negotiations continued. [34]

While these talks proceeded, Adams warned his Spanish counterpart that problems along the frontier might necessitate American intervention in Spanish territory. In Florida the Seminole Indians had continually raided across the international boundary into American territory. Pirates based along the coast of Texas were creating a hazard to American shipping. By the Treaty of San Lorenzo of 1795, Spain had promised to control the natives of its territories and to prevent their injuring United States citizens. Adams warned that Spain was not fulfilling this agreement. General Andrew Jackson, military commander of the southern area of the United States, had already been given broad powers to punish the offending Seminoles. [35] Onís was not impressed by Adams's arguments.

On January 16, 1818, Adams and Onís again met to discuss the affair. Adams proposed setting the Colorado River as a western boundary for Louisiana and the cession of all Spanish territory east of the Mississippi to the United States, in return for the Americans giving up a claim to Texas. Onís's reply was to ask whether Adams was referring to the Colorado of Natchitoches, one of the Spanish names for the Red River. Surely, Onís said, Adams could not be speaking of the Colorado River that flowed through the middle of the Spanish province. Whether the Spaniard was attempting to cloud the issue or to chide Adams for his boldness in demanding Spanish territory is unclear. In his report to Spain, Onís seemed certain which river the Americans meant. [36]

Finally, in April, Onís was ordered to offer the Americans a compromise: Spain would cede the Floridas to the United States, settling the eastern boundary dispute. As the western boundary a line would be drawn between Natchitoches and Los Adaes straight north to the Missouri River, follow that stream to its source, and proceed straight north again. The proposal would at least allow the beginning of give-and-take negotiations. This was the moment for which John Quincy Adams had been waiting. But before Onís forwarded these proposals to Adams the diplomats were shocked by news from the frontier—Andrew Jackson had invaded Florida.[37]

Onís was looking forward to the end of the cold, wet winter when news of Jackson's invasion reached him, spoiling his good spirits. He immediately issued protests to the American government. Despite the uproar that Jackson's bold action produced, the action provided the incentive needed to spur the diplomats to serious negotiating. After the frontier move, both Onís and Adams realized that a settlement to the affair was needed quickly to avoid further incident—possibly even war between the United States and Spain. Neither Adams nor Onís wanted war.[38]

In October, after the furor over Jackson's invasion had abated slightly, the Spaniard made new proposals. Florida would be ceded to the United States, as had been previously proposed. In the west the Spaniards were willing to compromise further. A line would be drawn following the Arroyo Hondo as before, but it would follow the course of the Red River to 32° north latitude and then run north to the Missouri and west along that stream's course. It was a small concession, but it was something. Finally, fifteen years after the Louisiana Purchase had been made, negotiations to settle the disputed boundary began in earnest.[39]

Adams rejected the Spanish offer but countered with his own proposal. The cession of Florida had become assured except for Spanish land grants that had been made in that region. The problem was negotiating Louisiana's western boundary. Adams proposed that a line be drawn running up the Sabine River from its mouth to the 32d parallel, north to the Red, up that stream to its source, north to the 42d parallel, and west along that degree line to the Pacific Ocean. This proposal, Adams told Onís, was the final American offer. Spain could accept these terms, or negotiations would end.[40] The Spaniard demurred. In mid-November, he announced new Spanish terms: the line would begin at the Sabine, but would go straight north to the Missouri and along that river to its source. In the period preceding Adams's offer and Onís's reply, the Spaniard received permission from his government to withdraw Spanish claims to the Colorado River. Onís evidently believed that he could make an agreement without yielding part of Texas and concealed this news from Adams.[41]

The negotiations were delayed by other events. The primary obstacles to progress were twofold: (1) Spanish demands that the United States make reparations for the damage done by Jackson's invasion and that the general receive a public reprimand and (2) the fall of Pizarro's ministry because of financial troubles and intrigue at the royal court. Adams refused to admit any wrongdoing by Jackson, arguing that the invasion was helpful to Spain because it punished the Seminoles. When the Marquís de Casa Irujo became prime minister and continued the policy of allowing Onís a free hand, the negotiations resumed.[42]

After Onís received his new instructions from Irujo, and after Adams laid to rest the dispute over Jackson's invasion, the two men were near a settlement. On February 1, 1819, the Spaniard issued a revised offer to Adams, embodying new and liberal compromise terms. A line would be drawn up the Sabine to its source, run north to the Red River, follow that stream to the 95th meridian, go straight north to the Arkansas and along that stream to its source, run due west to the Willamette, and follow that river to the Pacific. Of course, the Willamette, a tributary of the Columbia, did not flow into the Pacific, but neither Adams nor Onís had specific information concerning the geography of the West. The agreement worked on paper and for their purposes proved satisfactory.[43]

The Americans rejected Onís's proposal, however, and issued a counterproposal. Adams suggested that the line be placed either on the 101st or 102d meridian, run north to the 41st parallel, and then move west along that line to the Pacific. Onís responded by offering to fix the boundary by starting along the Sabine north to the 32d parallel, run due north to the Red, run up that stream to the 100th meridian, turn north to the Arkansas, go up that stream to the 42d parallel, go west to the Willamette, follow that river to the 43d parallel, and continue west to the Pacific. Again inaccurate geographical information prevented the diplomats from realizing that the Arkansas did not touch the 42d parallel.[44]

President Monroe expressed pleasure at the terms, noting that a settlement seemed near. John Quincy Adams, however, was dissatisfied because the agreement did not include the cession of Texas to the United States. Yet Monroe was insistent that the dispute be settled.[45]

The treaty was signed on February 22, 1819, with minor changes. Florida was ceded to the United States in return for that nation's assumption of debts owed by Spain to American citizens. The western Louisiana boundary was similar to that proposed by Onís: it began at the mouth of the Sabine River, followed the west or south bank of the Sabine to the 32d parallel, ran due north to the Red River, followed that stream along its south or west bank to the 100th meridian, moved straight north to the Arkansas, ran west along that river to its source, then went due north to the 42d parallel, and continued due west to the Pacific Ocean. The boundary was placed on the southern or western banks of the streams mentioned at Adams's demand. He had been forced to give up his claims to Texas; therefore he demanded that Spain in return grant sole ownership of the rivers to the United States. It appeared to be a small matter, for Spaniards retained the right to navigate the streams; however, Adams's insistence on the south or west bank would later create many problems for the state of Texas in disputes over mineral rights in the beds of the Sabine and Red rivers. Also included in the treaty were minor settlements of claims and damage suits and assurances of protection of the rights of Spanish citizens living in the ceded territories.[46]

The Adams-Onís Treaty, as it became known, was greeted with loud protests because it did not secure Texas for the United States. Henry Clay led some officials who wanted to reject the treaty because Adams had forsaken all American claim to Texas, but there was little hope of success for the treaty's opponents. Adams had negotiated the first agreement that extended American ownership to the Pacific. The agreement also defined the southern and western boundaries of the Louisiana Purchase. The vagueness of Louisiana had become a festering sore by 1819. Settlers wishing to move into the area along the Red River could not be certain whether they were on American or Spanish soil until the boundary was drawn. Therefore, whatever the drawbacks of the treaty, its ratification was inevitable. Although disputes over the fate of Spanish land grants in Florida delayed the exchange of ratifications until 1821, the agreement withstood criticism. The United States once more had definite borders in the Southwest, and once more the Red River had an important role. The Red had separated Spanish and French possessions in the New World for more than half a century; in 1819 it marked the division of Spanish Texas and the United States. With this new agreement the area along the Red River was open for willing settlers to carve homes in the wilderness.[47]

6.

The Great Raft

When the Adams-Onís Treaty was signed in 1819, the lower valley of the Red River below the Great Raft was rapidly being settled by Americans. Alexandria, near the mouth of the river, and Natchitoches, the old French trading post, had become centers of trade and marketing. Rapides Parish, where Alexandria was located, had 6,065 citizens in the census of 1820, while Natchitoches County had 7,486 inhabitants that year. Between the two towns were farmers cutting timber and selling it to lumbermen, grubbing out stumps, and planting their fields with cotton. Traders still wandered the region selling goods at isolated farmhouses and bartering for furs with the few Indians still living there. Louisiana was booming, thanks in part to statehood, which had come in 1812, and the northern portion was gaining population rapidly.[1]

Upriver from the Great Raft, however, the valley of the Red River was still largely the domain of Indians in 1819, as it had been for uncountable centuries. Before that time few Americans had ventured into the area because national ownership of the region was uncertain. When the Adams-Onís Treaty removed that problem, three barriers to settlement remained: the land south of the Red was controlled by Spaniards until 1821 and then by Mexicans, whose policies toward American settlers fluctuated rapidly; the land north of the Red was forbidden to white settlers because it had been set aside by the United States government as a permanent home for Indians, many of them refugees from the East; and the Great Raft was blocking navigation of the river and flooding the surrounding countryside with backwater. Before the upper portion of the Red could be settled permanently, each of these barriers had to be modified drastically.[2]

As early as 1763, when Spain received Louisiana from France, Spaniards realized that the vast, sprawling province should be populated. But how to populate the area was a difficult problem. Despite repeated attempts by the Spanish government to encourage its citizens to colonize Louisiana, few Spaniards were willing to forsake civilization for the wilderness. After the American Revolution, however, some citizens of the new republic were lured across the Mississippi by a Spanish promise of free or inexpensive land. At first Spanish officials were favorable to the colonization of Louisiana by Americans, but they gradually grew fearful that Americans were plotting to wrest the province from Spanish control. Their fear was heightened by the French Revolution, which caused the death of many aristocrats in Europe and had many supporters in the United States. Most Spanish officials were noblemen and uninspired by the freethinking republicanism espoused by revolutionaries. Indeed, many Spaniards, while fingering their ruffled collars, saw American colonists as potential revolutionaries. In 1795 all foreigners were banned from the Spanish colonies—and all Frenchmen were ordered to be arrested.[3]

After the Louisiana Purchase, Spanish officials in Texas became increasingly suspicious of the intentions of Americans who wished to enter the province. They believed that the grasping attitude of the Americans concerning the boundaries of Louisiana indicated rampant imperialism toward Spanish colonies. Thus Texas was closed to Americans in 1804 by order of Commandant General Nemesio Salcedo.[4]

The passage of time gradually relieved these fears of American aggression, although several filibusters in Texas during the second decade of the nineteenth century had come from the United States. By 1820, Spanish officials were again concerned about the scant population in Texas. Any fears they had were overcome by desire to populate the province. Thus in late 1820 they were receptive to the plan of Moses Austin to bring American settlers into Texas, although they were careful to assure the loyalty of such Americans by demanding from them an oath of allegiance.[5]

The creation of the Indian Territory, accompanied by prohibition of white settlement of the area, kept whites out of the Red River valley in present-day Oklahoma. The policy of the United States toward Indians led to the construction above Natchitoches of the first military post on the Red River. Hoping to prevent conflicts among the Indians, the United States Army established Cantonment Towson near the confluence of the Red and Kiamichi rivers in May, 1824. A small garrison was stationed at the post to keep the peace, but the need for the troops elsewhere and the difficulties of supplying the post caused by the raft on the Red River forced the cantonment to be abandoned in 1829.[6]

After Cantonment Towson was abandoned, trouble with the Indians increased. A year after the troops left the post on the Red, they returned there to establish Camp Phoenix. The post was opened in November, 1830; in 1831 it was renamed Cantonment Towson, the name given to the original post at the site. In the same year the army also established Cantonment Leavenworth, farther upriver on the Red near the mouth of the Washita.[7]

The establishment of the two military posts accentuated the need for the removal of the Great Raft from the Red River. Boats carrying supplies to these posts were forced to circumnavigate the raft by entering the bayous and cutoffs along the course of the river, extending the time needed to make the voyage and endangering the vessels and their cargoes. The time had come for the government to begin the long-awaited effort to remove the obstruction from the river.[8]

Many people had urged the government to remove the raft. The advantages to be gained by its removal were obvious. Of course, the primary gain would be easier navigation of the Red River. Cleared of this obstruction, the river would become a highway for commerce and settlement of the interior of the continent. That alone was justification for the necessary appropriations to remove the raft. Other advantages were probable. The raft clogged the river to the extent that water that ordinarily would have flowed harmlessly downstream was backed up, flooding the lowlands on either side of the river. Thus large areas of present-day northeast Texas, northwest Louisiana, southwest Arkansas, and southeast Oklahoma were inundated annually. The lands were fertile and ideal for farming, but could not be settled because of the high waters created by the raft.[9]

Removal of the raft could occur only after Congressional action. Andrew H. Sevier, a leader of the Arkansas delegation, presented several documents to Congress containing information about the raft. They were the first detailed reports that Congress received concerning the problem. One of the reports was especially informative because it came from Joseph Paxton, of Mount Prairie, Arkansas, in the southwest part of the territory. Paxton, a long-term resident of the region and a trained scientist, detailed the problems that the raft had created and suggested methods for its removal.[10] To Sevier he wrote:

Opening the raft, then, would reclaim at least three-fourths of the land at present occupied, and rendered entirely useless by it [the water], and thus would place at the immediate disposal of the United States, property in its present situation of no value, but which would then be worth the enormous sum of seven hundred thousand dollars.[11]

Realizing that congressmen might be skeptical of such a large figure, Paxton explained his calculations:

The raft is eighty miles long, and will average twenty in width. This section . . . would be more completely reclaimed, and when reclaimed, would be better, inasmuch as it would be more free from inundation, than the bottoms of this river generally; and the numerous lakes in this valley that formed by the river so frequently cutting across the necks of its bends, are filled up.—These circumstances, together with its advantageous situation in other respects, would render it equal, if not superior, in intrinsic value, to any section of its size whatever.[12]

Paxton tried to convince the national legislators that removal of the raft was in the national interest: "Opening the raft would prevent an immense destruction of United States' property. It must not be forgotten that the raft is not standing still, but is gradually progressing upwards, like a destroying angel, spreading desolation over a most lovely country."[13] The growth of the raft was costing "the appalling rate of near one hundred thousand dollars in each ten years."[14] Moreover, wrote Paxton, the raft was impeding the settlement of the area behind it, leaving tens of thousands of beautiful, fertile acres desolate, with so few people that they hardly constituted "three respectable counties." Next he appealed to American patriotism, asserting that if the raft was not removed the region upriver would remain under the influence of Spaniards and Indians.[15]

Fearing that his congressional readers might not fully understand the advantages of appropriating funds for the removal of the raft, he summarized the benefits that would follow. Among them were easier transport for supplies bound for Cantonment Towson and greater control over the Indians living along the upper Red River. These two elements were directly linked. At the time of his writing, Paxton knew that Army officials were considering the removal of the soldiers from Cantonment Towson because of difficulties in supplying them. Such a removal, he declared, would be a grave mistake; more troops were needed, not fewer. Angrily he wrote that the government "as well might send a bear in pursuit of an antelope, as troops after the Osages."[16]

Finally Paxton asserted that lumber along the Red River

that would be available once the raft was removed would be worth the expenditure. He wrote:

About forty miles above the head of the raft it [the forest] commences growing, and seems to take place and grow in the same kinds of soil that the cypress does below. It would be difficult for a person acquainted only with upland cedars, to form a correct idea of the beauty, size, and symmetry of those that grow in the bottoms of Red River. I have seen, with wonder and never-ceasing astonishment, those vast, lofty cedar groves, in many places for three hundred miles above the settlement. They had frequently been described to me, but I had formed no adequate idea of them; nor do I believe it is in the power of language to give a representation of their imposing grandeur, that would not fall far short of reality on seeing them. They would doubtless be a valuable acquisition, particularly to the Navy, and to the city and neighborhood of New-Orleans; nor can I believe that the time is far hence, when the cedars of Red river will become as celebrated in these United States, as those of Lebanon were once in Palestine.[17]

After praising the virtues of opening the Red River, Paxton turned to the matter of performing the task. Although he begged congressmen to realize that he was not an expert concerning cost analysis, he asserted, "Opening the raft, however, would doubtless far more than remunerate government for any money that, with proper management, would be necessarily expended."[18] He suggested several ways of removing the raft, such as cutting canals to divert the waters of the Red into old channels that had been forsaken by the whims of the river. After the water was diverted, the riverbed could then be cleared of the raft. He also suggested that the bayous and swamps along the river should be dammed to prevent the formation of another raft, because much of the driftwood which had formed the original raft had come into the stream from these sources. Finally, low banks that were likely to be washed away by high waters should be built up to prevent such an occurrence. Paxton concluded that the raft should be removed as soon as possible for the sake of the nation, as well as the area along the river.[19]

The first congressional appropriation for the removal of the raft, made on May 23, 1828, was $25,000—a miniscule sum considering the magnitude of the task at hand. For the next four years little was done except planning. In 1832, Captain Henry Miller Shreve of the Army Corps of Engineers, the first captain to take a steamboat above the rapids at Alexandria by ascending the Red in the *Enterprise* in 1815, was appointed to direct the removal of the obstruction. At the time of his appointment, Shreve was superintendent of the Western Waters Department of the corps. Originally, the corps had planned to circumvent the raft by digging canals and deepening bayous rather than clearing the main channel. By 1832, however, the Army's chief engineer, Brigadier General Charles Gratiot, had determined that the plan "of opening short canals and deepening bayous with a view to effect a passage around the raft, is not such as to ensure permanent benefit."[20] Gratiot therefore wrote to Shreve, asking him to reappraise the situation.[21]

On September 29, 1832, Captain Shreve replied to Gratiot that "by the application of the proper means to accomplish such an object . . . the raft may be removed at much less expense than canals can be excavated . . . and better navigation would of course be obtained."[22] Shreve suggested that the raft could be removed easily if all obstructions below it were cleared. The timbers of the raft could be loosened and allowed to float downstream. This not only would facilitate the removal of the raft but also would improve the navigability of the lower section of the stream. Finally, Shreve suggested that the task could be performed by the snag boat *Archimedes*, which he had designed. At that time it was working on the Ohio River.[23]

Evidently impressed by Shreve's ideas, General Gratiot on February 8, 1833, ordered the captain to proceed with all available machinery to the Red River and to commence oper-

94

ations to remove the raft. After a short delay, created by his absence from the corps's western headquarters in Louisville, Kentucky, Shreve departed for the Red River, arriving at the Great Raft on April 11, 1833.[24]

Shreve related his first impression of the raft when he reported to Gratiot. He wrote that he had traveled five miles into the raft and had found it surprisingly easy to remove. He noted that the serious problem would be disposing of the timber after it had been removed from the raft. He wrote, "It is impracticable to clear the banks of the timber and willows that grow to low water mark" because of the water level in the river. He added hopefully that if this problem was solved the raft could be cleared away in two months.[25]

A month after his first report to Gratiot, Shreve wrote that about forty miles of the raft had been cleared. Thirty-one sections of the raft had been removed "by drawing them out, log by log, and separating them in such manner as to pass them down the bayous." He continued that the bayous were filled with logs and then were packed solid when a snag boat was rammed against them. Thus two problems were solved. The unwanted timbers were disposed of, and the bayous were filled, preventing runoff water from entering the main channel.[26]

On June 23, 1833, progress ceased because of low water. During the three months of work four snag boats, the *Archimedes*, the *Souvenir*, the *Java*, and the *Pearl*, had removed more than seventy miles of the raft. Shreve happily reported that the main channel was deepening because of the increased current created by the removal of the raft and the closing of the bayous. Shreve, evidently secure in his methods, ended his report by declaring that he was "prepared to state to the department, in positive terms, that the whole of the great raft can be removed in such a manner as to be as permanent and safe a steamboat navigation as any part of the river, from the raft to the Mississippi."[27] All that was needed was congressional funds.

In his report to the Chief Engineer, detailing the work done during fiscal year 1833, Shreve noted that "the expense of removing the raft . . . will be repaid at least threefold by the lands that must evidently be redeemed in the immediate line of the raft."[28] He asked that Congress appropriate $100,000 to complete the task.[29]

The national legislators responded to Shreve's request by allotting $50,000 for the project, and work continued the next season. To the dismay of Shreve and his superiors, the raft had replenished itself during the off-season. While the engineers had been prevented from working, low waters had continued to deposit driftwood in the main channel. In addition, several dams that had been built in the bayous had rotted and broken, allowing timbers to return to the raft and water to drain from the main channel. The problems of removing the raft were greater than Shreve had originally supposed.[30]

Although Shreve had estimated that the raft could be removed for $100,000, costs continued to mount. In 1835, Congress again allotted $50,000, bringing the total appropriation to Shreve's original figure of $100,000. Still, work was not completed on the raft. Additional apropriations of $40,000 in 1836, $65,000 in 1837, and $75,000 in 1838 were necessary to continue the task.[31] Despite this large outlay of funds, the raft remained.

In December, 1839, Captain Abram Tyson, commanding the snag boat *Eradicator* and accompanied by a keelboat and a large group of men, reached the raft to begin operations. Removal work continued until April 15, when "an unusual high freshet in the river brought down a heavy run of timber, and formed a new raft of 2,150 yards in the same place from which the original raft had been removed."[32] This new raft blocked the channel entirely, trapping two steamboats on the upper section of the stream. By June, 1839, all appropriated funds had been expended. Almost a quarter of a million dollars had been spent, and the river was still blocked by the contrary raft. Shreve, still in charge of the operation, estimated that another $85,000 was needed to complete the task.[33]

Shreve evidently realized that congressmen were growing unhappy with the continued expense involved in removing the raft. In his report for fiscal year 1839 he added another list of advantages that would be obtained by removing it. Congressmen were unimpressed, and no funds were appropriated in 1839 or 1840. Work on the raft stopped—and the obstruction grew. In December, 1839, Quartermaster General Thomas Jesup informed Secretary of War Joel Poinsett that supplies for Fort Towson would have to be transported overland because the raft made navigation of the Red River impossible. By the end of 1839 the raft had grown a mile in length. More than $200,000 and five years of work would be negated by the whims of the river unless action was taken. [34]

Everyone realized that work had to be resumed to remove the raft. Finally, in September, 1841, Congress appropriated $75,000 for the project. The burden of directing removal of the raft had passed from Shreve to Colonel Stephen Harriman Long, an experienced engineer and scientist who had led an expedition into the trans-Mississippi West twenty years before his appointment. In the spring of 1841, Long took command of operations on Red River. [35]

On reaching the Red, Long found the same difficulties that Shreve had faced. They included constant additions to the raft made by each rise of the water and the disposal of timber that had been extracted from the raft. Work on the raft was limited to six months each year, from January to June, because of a marked decrease in the depth of the water during the summer and fall. While the water was low, the river was flooded by sporadic rains on its upper watershed. The dramatic rising and falling of the water left large deposits of driftwood, enlarging the raft. Also, the timber that had been placed in bayous rotted and escaped, reentering the raft. The problems had been compounded by repeated delays in repairing aging machinery. Colonel Long reported that on arriving at the raft he had found the snag boat *Eradicator* "lying at the shore of the river out of repair, and unfit for service." [36] The failure of Con-

97

Colonel Stephen H. Long. A noted explorer of the American west and a
well-trained engineer, Long found the Red River a worthy opponent. Courtesy the National Archives.

gress to appropriate funds for the project had prevented proper maintenance.

By Long's estimation, $75,000 was needed for the removal of the raft. His report contained no promises of early completion and immediate benefits. The Red River raft had become a complex and challenging problem not to be taken lightly. Long realized that many more dollars and man-hours would be needed to open the river. [37]

Although Congress answered Long's request by appropriating $75,000 in 1841, little progress was made. Problems with the raft continued to negate the efforts of the engineers. Hoping to facilitate the task, Long turned to private contractors. In 1841, Thomas T. Williamson was contracted to remove three miles of the raft for $15,000. Additional funds were provided for keeping the river open for four years. [38]

Williamson's contract granted him the right to dig artificial channels across bends of the river. Thus the river would be straightened, and the loops of the bends could be used to store unwanted timber from the raft. Residents of the river below the raft complained, however, that the cutoffs would increase both the volume and the speed of the river's current, flooding their lands and ruining their crops. As a result, Williamson was not allowed to create artificial channels. The change in plans increased expenses and slowed progress. Although the work was completed during the spring of 1842, the cost of removing three miles of raft was considerably more than $15,000. Then a large freshet of water late in the spring brought great quantities of driftwood downriver after the work was completed, creating a raft larger than the one that had been removed. The work had to be done again. [39]

Williamson continued laboring on the raft until 1845. That year the superintendent of the project, Captain Charles Linnard, wrote:

Work of this kind cannot be done by contract. He who has sufficient means will not hazard them in so precious and costly an undertaking and he who has not is, of course, unable to accomplish anything. Such work can be done only by the Government, with its own means, and under well-selected superintendents. It is not merely necessary that the materials of which they are composed be . . . destroyed.[40]

Thus the experiment in using private contractors to remove the Red River raft ended in failure. Most of the funds that had been appropriated in 1841 had been expended by 1845, and Congress was unwilling to make additional allotments. Removal of the raft slowed to a standstill. Work was resumed briefly in 1852, when, reacting to public demand, Congress appropriated $100,000. Colonel Joseph E. Johnston was appointed to command the project. The thrust of the work consisted of constructing canals around the raft. Continued failures to develop a permanent solution soon brought efforts to a halt.[41]

Work resumed under the direction of Charles A. Fuller, a civilian agent of the Army Corps of Topographical Engineers. By 1855 only $6,000 of the appropriation had been spent. Fuller's report for 1855 gave little hope of a permanent solution to the problem. His suggestions were limited to annual expenditures for the removal of each new raft that formed with the rising water. Thus the project had deteriorated from permanently improving the Red River for navigation to repeatedly removing the obstructions each year. The river would be open for navigation only a few months each year and an annual appropriation would be necessary. Congress was unwilling to see huge amounts of government funds float down the Red River each year and refused further appropriations. The nation was descending into the greatest crisis of its history, and national legislators were too busy with debates over slavery and transcontinental railroad routes to be concerned with inland waterways, especially one that had proven so expensive and uncooperative as the Red River. Congress would not appropriate additional funds for the removal of the raft until 1872, long after the problems of the 1850s had been solved by war and replaced by other questions.[42]

Although the first effort to remove the raft had failed, much of the upper Red River valley had been settled by 1855. A revolution in 1836 had ended the problem of Mexican ownership of Texas, and its subsequent annexation by the United States had led to the migration of many Americans to the area along the south bank of the Red. The north bank of the river had been populated by members of the Choctaw and Chicksaw nations; the white populations of both Louisiana and Arkansas had increased measurably, reaching more than 30,000 and 20,000 respectively in 1850. In the 1830s Shreveport, Louisiana, had grown on the west bank of the Red about one hundred miles north of Natchitoches. Jefferson, Texas, founded in the 1830s on Big Cyprus Creek fifty miles from the Red River, had become one of the leading towns in Texas, with a population of more than five thousand by 1850. Also by 1850, Jefferson was a leading water port—because of the raft. With the raft clogging the main channel, backed-up waters of the stream raised the level sufficiently to allow steamboats to reach Jefferson. Because of this Jefferson was the trading center of northeast Texas. The prosperity that Jefferson enjoyed, however, was tied to its relation with the Red. Removal of the raft would stop the shipment of goods and end the years of plenty.

Despite the growth of the population of the Red River valley, in 1850 the section west of the 97th meridian remained desolate, the home of the unchallenged masters of the southern plains, the Comanches. Since 1800 the area west of the 97th meridian had remained unchanged. The bison still roamed the land and provided food for the natives, and the Comanches still swept down from their homes along the Red River to spread destruction across Texas. Thomas Jefferson's dream of an American expedition to the source of the Red

River remained unfulfilled. In 1852, Randolph B. Marcy set out on one of the last great explorations of the American West to discover the headwaters of the Red River—and to still Jefferson's ghost.

7.

Randolph Marcy
and the "Terra Incognita"

By mid-nineteenth century, the United States had expanded across North America and reached from the Atlantic to the Pacific, from Canada to Mexico. From New York to California, Americans could call the land theirs. The United States was coming of age, but despite the refinement of Boston and the bustle of San Francisco, much of the region stretching from the Mississippi to the Rockies and from Texas to the Dakota country lay unknown and unsettled, guarding its secrets from white men. Zebulon Pike and John C. Frémont had crossed the American West, but much of what Jefferson had bought in 1803 remained unknown to whites.

Thomas Jefferson had organized two expeditions to ascend the Red River to its source. Both had failed. Zebulon Pike set out across the West in 1805 to discover the sources of the Arkansas and Red rivers. He failed mainly because of problems of his own making. In 1820, Stephen Harriman Long, a dour and scholarly explorer, mistook the Canadian for the Red. The upper reaches of the Red River remained the domain of Indians. That situation could not be allowed to continue. The Red River, once an important international boundary and, in 1850, the northern border of Texas, could not remain unknown to its owners. The task of making it known fell to Captain Randolph Barnes Marcy of the U.S. Fifth Infantry.[1]

Randolph Marcy was born in Greenwich, Massachusetts, in 1812, and graduated from the United States Military Academy

103

twenty years later. In 1849 he guided a group of two thousand westering settlers from Fort Smith, Arkansas, to Santa Fe, New Mexico, blazing a trail along the South Canadian as he went. The endeavor won Marcy acclaim for his talents, along with further assignments as an explorer. From 1849 to 1852, Marcy explored the region around the headwaters of the Trinity, Brazos, and Colorado rivers of Texas. During that period he noticed

the remarkable fact that a portion of one of the largest and most important rivers in the United States . . . remained unexplored and unknown, no white man having ever ascended the stream [the Red River] to its sources. . . . In a word, the country embraced within the basin of Upper Red River had always been to us a "terra incognita." [2]

On March 5, 1852, Randolph Marcy was instructed by Congress to remedy this situation. [3]

Marcy was urged to make his exploration without unnecessary delay. He proceeded to the Red River, arriving near the mouth of the Little Wichita River in May, 1852. Brevet Captain George B. McClellan, a close friend and his future son-in-law, was his second-in-command. Supplies were shipped overland by wagons from Fort Smith, Arkansas, to the mouth of Cache Creek, the official starting point of the expedition. Marcy, McClellan, and a small contingent of soldiers followed the Red from the mouth of the Little Wichita to Cache Creek, arriving there on May 13. When he found that the supply train had not yet arrived because of heavy rains, Marcy explored the surrounding area. He was impressed by the plant life of the area, noting the size and quantity of trees. The next day the baggage train arrived, and the expedition began in earnest. [4]

The party followed the river westward. Soon they were excited by discovering buffalo tracks. Marcy remarked, "We are anxiously awaiting the time when we shall see the animals themselves, and anticipate much sport." [5] The Indians who had been hired as guides informed the party that the tracks were five days old and that the buffalo were far away. The sport would have to wait. That evening the explorers got an unwelcome surprise. One of the guides informed them that a cougar had crossed the river nearby and was heading toward their camp. The soldiers immediately set their hunting dogs loose. The dogs, elated to be free from their shackles, sprinted into the darkness. Marcy noted, however, that "the zeal which they manifested in starting out from camp, suddenly abated as soon as their 'olfactories' came in contact with the track." The soldiers pursuaded the rightfully cautious canines to continue, and the cougar was soon treed. Marcy arrived at the scene first and "fired several shots, which took effect and soon placed him 'hors de combat.'"[6] Marcy's first big-game trophy of the journey measured eight and a half feet from nose to tail.[7]

The next day rugged terrain forced the party to leave the river. In the afternoon the group was astonished by a freshet in a small stream. An hour after they found the stream empty except for occasional holes of water, it was brimming with a "perfect torrent." Marcy was amazed because the skies had been clear for several days; his Indian guides informed him that it was a gift from the Great Spirit.[8]

Soon the rains that had swollen the creek reached the party, drenching the men and delaying progress. On May 22 the group continued, having sighted the Wichita Mountains. That afternoon they reached a small tributary of the Red that they named Otter Creek in honor of the many inhabitants of the stream. A short excursion up this stream to its exit from the Wichitas revealed deposits of quartz containing small flakes of gold. The same deposits would lure latter-day prospectors to the region to search vainly for a mother lode.[9]

As delaying rains continued, Marcy concluded that, because the region was unusually dry, the effects of the Wichita Mountains protruding into the atmosphere created the heavy downpours. On May 26 the group sighted their first buffalo,

General Randolph B. Marcy, who was a Captain of the U.S. Fifth Infantry at the time he led the 1852 expedition to explore the Red River. Courtesy of the Western History Collections, University of Oklahoma Library.

and one of the beasts was killed by an Indian guide. Marcy noted that the country changed near the mountains, and the river, was different there; whereas it previously had been wide and slow moving, it now was a narrow, rushing torrent.[10]

On the twenty-seventh the explorers met a party of Wichita Indians who had been hunting buffalo. The natives had many horses loaded with meat and were bound for their villages. The chief told Marcy that he had been searching for the white men for several days, having heard of their presence and wanting to know of their business in his land. Marcy replied that he was going to the headwaters of the Red River and assured the chief of the peaceful intent of his mission. Gifts were also given to the natives. Marcy then warned the chief that the Republic of Texas had become part of the United States and that depredations in Texas would result in severe punishment for the offending Indians.[11]

After these preliminaries Marcy asked the chief for information about the country upriver. The reply was disheartening:

. . . we would find one more stream of good water about two days' travel . . . that we should then leave the mountains, and after that find no more fresh water to the sources of the river. The chief represented the river from where it leaves the mountains as flowing over an elevated flat prairie country, totally destitute of water, wood, or grass, and the only substitute for fuel that could be had was the buffalo "chips."[12]

Marcy then asked whether fresh-water holes could be found. The chief replied that all water soaked into the dry earth as soon as it fell from the sky.[13]

The natives left, but their information remained. The explorer wrote that "it would seem that we have anything but an agreeable prospect before us."[14] But he would not forsake his mission: "As soon . . . as the creek will admit of fording, I shall, without subjecting the command to too great privations, push forward as far as possible into this most inhospitable and dreaded salt desert."[15] Randolph Marcy had not received command of the expedition for timidity.[16]

The next day the explorers discovered by lunar observations that their camp was near the point "where the line dividing the Choctaw territory from the State of Texas crosses the Red River."[17] They marked the exact spot by carving the longitude (100° 0' 45") and latitude (34° 34' 6") on a convenient tree. The next day, May 29, McClellan found and marked the point where the 100th meridian crossed the Red River.[18] Unfortunately, these observations were later found to be in error, probably because of imperfections in the instruments used to calculate them, and the incorrect survey complicated a border dispute between Oklahoma and Texas many years later.

On May 30 the party marched to the confluence of the Red and its North Fork. Here the stream was 650 yards wide. After passing the confluence of the streams, the explorers progressed up the North Fork without hardship for two days, arriving at the mouth of a stream that Marcy called the Salt Fork (today's Elm Fork). The contents of this stream were brackish and salty, polluting the contents of the main channel. Also, the waters in the main stream were found to contain minerals and salts that made it unpalatable. Fresh-water springs were found, however, that provided sufficient quantities of drinking water. Near the mouth of the Salt Fork the party found a large mountain that they named Mount Webster in honor of Daniel Webster, the secretary of state.[19]

Ascending the North Fork, the party found signs of a hunting party of Comanche Indians; however, no natives were sighted. Marcy noted that his Delaware and Shawnee guides were enemies of the Comanches but that they scouted far away from the main column each day without fear. He remarked that they were ready to fight any Plains Indians if the odds were not greater than six to one.[20]

On June 7, Marcy and two of the Indian guides set out to explore the surrounding area. After traveling about three miles, the trio found fresh buffalo tracks. Marcy, still eager to make his first kill, decided to follow the tracks, hoping to overtake the animals. On reaching a rise, he sent one of his

General George B. McClellan, second-in-command to Marcy for the expedition in 1852, was Brevet Captain at that time. From *Battles and Leaders of the Civil War*, Volume 2 (New York, 1887). Courtesy of the Western History Collections, University of Oklahoma Library.

guides to the top to survey the area for animals. The guide, John Bull, rode to the appointed spot and began a series of gyrations that ended as he left at a full gallop toward the horizon. Marcy and his companion followed to the top of the rise, arriving in time to see Bull in hot pursuit of a fleeing buffalo. Marcy wrote that the native was:

mounted upon one of our most fractious and spirited horses, that had never seen a buffalo before, and coming near the animal he seemed perfectly frantic with fear, making several desperate surges to the right and left, any one of which must have inevitably unseated his rider had he not been a most expert and skillful horseman.[21]

As Bull drew near the beast, he emptied his rifle in its direction; however, the great animal continued his fast pace. Reloading as he rode, Bull pulled closer and "placed another ball directly back of the shoulder; but so tenacious of his life is this animal, that it was not until the other Delaware and myself arrived and gave him four additional shots, that we brought him to the ground."[22] The three took the best parts of the carcass and found a spring, which Marcy determined would be the site of the next camp.[23]

On the same day, Marcy dispatched McClellan with an interpreter to follow Comanche tracks found along the path. The party returned to report that the natives had departed southward.[24] The party then proceeded up the North Fork, sighting the Llano Estacado on June 12, 1852. That day the explorers camped near the remains of hunting lodges of a band of Kiowa Indians. The native guides told the white men that the camp had been Kiowa rather than Comanche, because the former dug "holes for their fires about two feet in diameter, while the latter only make them about fifteen inches."[25]

The party left the site and pushed farther upstream, reaching the headwaters on June 16. There the men buried a bottle containing a note that read in part:

On the 16th of June, 1852, an exploring expedition, composed of Captain R. B. Marcy, Captain G. B. McClellan, Lieutenant J. Updegraff, and Doctor G. C. Shumard, with fifty-five men of company D fifth infantry, encamped here, having traced the north branch of Red river to its source. [26]

A nearby tree was emblazoned with the message: "Exploring Expedition, June 16, 1852." [27] The first leg of the journey had been completed.

Marcy and eleven of his companions set out northward to find the Canadian River. After marching about twenty-five miles, the group arrived at the Canadian and soon found a point on the stream that Marcy recognized from his exploration in 1849. Having completed this mission, the party returned to the main camp. The next day, June 20, Marcy directed his men southward toward the main channel of the Red River—and its source. [28]

For six days the explorers traveled southward, sighting a party of Kiowas on the twenty-second but avoiding contact. On June 26 they reached a massive prairie-dog town, which Marcy calculated covered several hundred thousand square acres. He estimated "the holes to be at the usual distances of about twenty yards apart, and each burrow occupied by a family of four or five dogs. I fancy that the aggregate population would be greater than any other city in the universe." [29] Marcy, noting that it had been asserted that rattlesnakes and prairie dogs lived in harmony in the same holes, remarked "we have satisfied ourselves that this is a domestic arrangement entirely at variance with the wishes of the dogs, as the snakes prey upon them, and must be considered as intruders." [30] In support of this conclusion Marcy wrote that a rattlesnake killed by the explorers was found to have swallowed a full-grown prairie dog. [31]

Pulling himself away from his evident fascination with prairie dogs, Marcy pushed southward, skirting the edge of the Llano Estacado. On June 24 he reached the main channel of the Red near its exit from the Staked Plains. There the river was nine hundred yards wide, flowing over a sandy bed. The next day the group reached the Llano, looming eight hundred feet above the prairies. Marcy and McClellan attempted to blaze a trail up the escarpment that would allow passage for the wagons. This task proved to be futile, but the excursion did provide the explorers with excitement. [32]

During the brief survey of the area the two explorers sighted a herd of antelope grazing quietly in a stand of mesquite. Marcy, ever a hunter, wanted to call one of the animals within range of his rifle. He began a series of bleats with the call he had brought for such an occasion. One of the horned beasts approached. Marcy readied his weapon and was about to fire when his attention was captured by "a rustling which I heard in the grass to my left. Casting my eyes in that direction, to my no small astonishment I saw a tremendous panther bounding at full speed directly towards me, and within the short distance of twenty steps." [33] His role now changed from the hunter to the hunted. Marcy continued:

As may be imagined, I immediately abandoned the antelope, and directing my rifle at the panther, sent a ball through his chest, which stretched him out upon the grass about ten yards from where I had taken my position. Impressed with the belief that I had accomplished a feat of rather more than ordinary importance in the sporting line, I placed my hand to my mouth, ("a la savage,") and gave several as loud shouts of exultation as my weak lungs would admit, partly for the purpose of giving vent to my feelings of triumph, and also to call the Captain [McClellan]. [34]

The experience was not over. When McClellan approached and the two men returned to the spot of Marcy's feat, they found the prey "upon his feet, making off." [35] Acting quickly, McClellan discharged his rifle into the beast and administered a clubbing with the stock "to give him his quietus." [36] The adventure was over.

It is to the explorer's credit that he noted the following:

It occurred to me afterwards that it would not always be consistent with one's safety to use the deer-bleat unless we were perfectly cer-

"View Near Head of Red River," a drawing from *Explorations of the Red River of Louisiana in the Year 1852*, by Captain Randolph B. Marcy and Captain George B. McClellan (Washington, 1854). Courtesy of the Western History Collections, University of Oklahoma Library.

tain we should have our wits about us in the event of a panther or large bear (which is often the case) taking it into his head to give credence to the counterfeit." [37]

Marcy summed up the incident, writing, "The panther had probably heard the bleat, and was coming towards it with the pleasant anticipation of making his breakfast from a tender fawn; but, fortunately for me, I disappointed him." [38]

Because the terrain was too rugged to support the wagons, the main party was left behind the next day while Marcy, McClellan, and ten others pushed on to the Llano Estacado. Following the course of the river onto the Llano, the men were awed by the grandeur of the terrain. The great height of the escarpments encasing the river bed gave the explorers the feeling of walking into a massive tunnel. The walls of valley

were worn away, by the lapse of time and the action of the water, and the weather, into the most fantastic forms, that required but little effort of the imagination to convert into works of art, and all united in forming one of the grandest and most picturesque scenes that can be imagined.[39]

Marcy, as always ready to invoke his powers of description, wrote:

We all, with one accord, stopped and gazed with wonder and admiration upon the panorama which was for the first time exhibited to the eyes of civilized man. Occasionally might be seen a good representation of the towering walls of a castle of the feudal ages, with its giddy battlements pierced with loopholes, and its projecting watch-towers standing out in bold relief upon the azure ground of pure and transparent sky above. In other places our fancy would metamorphose the escarpments into a bastion front, as perfectly modeled and constructed as if it had been a production of the genius of Vauban, with redoubts and salient angles all arranged in due order. Then, again, we would see a colossal specimen of sculpture representing the human figure, with all the features of the face, which, standing upon its lofty pedestal, overlooks the valley, and seems to have been designed and executed by the Almighty artist as the presiding genius of these dismal solitudes.[40]

Marcy was aware of the power—and possible danger—of nature. He saw hidden within the grandeur and beauty of nature "its unreclaimed sublimity and wildness," and the power and scope of the scene inspired him "with that veneration which is justly due to the high antiquity of nature's handiworks, and which seems to increase as we consider the solemn and important lesson that is taught us in reflecting upon their continued permanence when contrasted with our own fleeting and momentary existence."[41]

Despite their wonderment at the beauty of the area, the ex-

"Head of Ke-Che-Ah-Que-Ho-No, or Main Branch of Red River," a drawing from *Explorations of the Red River of Louisiana in the Year 1852*, by Captain
Randolph B. Marcy and Captain George B. McClellan (Washington,
1854). Courtesy of the Western History Collections, University of Oklahoma Library.

plorers suffered. On the Llano fresh water was scarce. Several soldiers attempted to drink the brackish, mineral-laden waters of the river, but were rewarded by severe stomach cramps and vomiting. Nonetheless, the men retained their cheerfulness, discussing "the relative merits of different kinds of fancy iced drinks that could be procured in the cities, and the prices that could be obtained for some of them if they were within reach of our party."[42] Even at night the group suffered. Sleep was an elusive goal despite the hardships of the day. Marcy noted that his "slumbers were continually disturbed by dreams, in which I fancied myself swallowing huge draughts of ice water."[43] One of the group offered two thousand dollars for one bucket of cold, clear water. Marcy sadly replied that "this was one of those few instances in which money was not sufficiently potent to attain the object desired."[44]

On July 1 the determination of the explorers was rewarded by the discovery of a fresh-water spring—and the source of the Red River. After refreshing themselves at the spring, the party proceeded to a place where the valley closed, uniting the walls of the escarpment. A spring burst "out from its cavernous reservoir, and, leaping down over the huge masses of rock below, here commences its long journey to unite with other tributaries in making the Mississippi the noblest river in the universe."[45] The men blazed a nearby tree with the date. Marcy had seen the headwaters of the Red River. More important to him and his men at the moment was the fresh, sweet water that trickled from the ground, quenching their thirst.[46]

Two days after finding the source of the river, the party returned to the main camp. On July 4, 1852, the explorers "turned our faces toward home."[47] Captain McClellan found a large cougar while riding ahead of the main party. He killed the cat with one shot, either by luck or by skill, bringing the group's total feline trophies to three. The rest of the journey proved uneventful, and on July 28 the explorers marched into the confines of Fort Arbuckle, Indian Territory.[48]

Marcy had completed his task. He had found the sources of

the main channel and the north fork of the Red River. Moreover, he had fulfilled his job without loss of life, and, as he also noted, the animals that were taken on the exploration were returned "in fine condition, and are now much better capable of performing service than when they came into our hands."[49]

The mission had been performed in the peace and serenity of nature, but the country to which the explorers returned was boiling with hatred and fear. While one of Jefferson's dreams was becoming reality, the nation that he had helped create was bursting at its seams.

8.

Highway of War

In April, 1861, civil war burst upon the United States. The nation seemed suddenly to have gone mad, allowing itself to be destroyed by southern fire-eaters and northern abolitionists. The conflict, however, had been long brewing. Slavery had troubled the nation since Washington's administration, and the struggle between the sections had grown steadily worse. The dispute over Missouri's entrance into the Union was, as John Quincy Adams wrote, "the first page of a tragic drama," and the Compromise of 1820 was a stopgap measure rather than a solution to the problem of the extension of slavery into western territories. The debate about the tariff in the early 1830s had led the nation to the brink of war; the Compromise of 1850 had prevented war while making no one happy. In 1854 the Kansas-Nebraska Act, establishing popular sovereignty in the western territories, had brought bloodshed to Kansas, and the Supreme Court's refusal of Dred Scott's plea for freedom had made compromise an evil word.

After 1820 the southern states had grown increasingly fearful of federal infringement of their rights, and by 1850 South Carolina was proclaiming to the world that it had not lost its sovereignty by joining the Union. Should the nation follow a course detrimental to South Carolina's welfare, leaders in that state felt that they were within their rights by seceding. South Carolina had joined the Union by choice; it could leave in the same manner. The North denied this assertion, replying that the Union was inviolate. When Abraham Lincoln, a Republican who had made known his views on slavery, was elected to the presidency in 1860, South Carolina exercised its self-proclaimed right to secede and demanded that all federal possessions in the state be turned over to its officials. Lincoln refused, and on April 19, 1861, the "More Perfect Union" fragmented into warring factions, torn by hatreds as old as the nation.

Both Confederates and Yankees believed that the war would be brief. Bull Run was followed by Shiloh, and mothers and wives wept because of deaths at strange-sounding places like Cold Harbor and Island No. 10. The nation soon learned the true meaning of civil war.

By the end of 1863 the Deep South was starving, strangled by the Union "Anaconda." Lincoln had blockaded the coast of the South during the first year of the war, and the fall of Vicksburg late in the spring of 1863 had given the North control of the Mississippi, cutting off supplies from the West. It seemed only a matter of time until the South would be forced to capitulate. How long would it be? How many more men would die?

After the fall of Vicksburg, General Ulysses S. Grant, commander of Union forces in the trans-Mississippi West, and General Nathaniel Prentiss Banks, commander of the Department of the Gulf, believed that Mobile, Alabama, should be the next target for a concerted Union assault. President Lincoln and Commanding General of the Army Henry W. ("Old Brains") Halleck did not agree. The South was surrounded, and Union armies were slicing into the heartland of the Confederacy. One state in the Confederacy, however, stood scarred but unconquered—Texas. Lincoln and Halleck, under the urgings of exiled Unionists from the state, such as Andrew Jackson Hamilton, believed that the establishment of Union supremacy in the Lone Star State was an urgent need to assure a quick end to the war. The psychological benefits from a successful invasion would be many, while an end to the trade between Texas and Mexico would deny Confederates in the

West a major source of supplies. Besides, the disturbing news of the arrival of French troops in Mexico in June, 1863, created fears of an arrangement between France and Texas—possibly the annexation of the state to France. Union conquest would preclude any such agreement, and it would strengthen the American position with regard to France's violation of the Monroe Doctrine in Mexico. Also, huge quantities of cotton were stored in Texas—more than enough to ease the shortages in the textile mills of the North.

With these goals in mind, Lincoln and his military chief urged Banks, who had more than thirty thousand men under his command, to plan and execute an invasion of Texas. Halleck advised Banks that the invasion would "be best and most safely effected by a combined military and naval movement up the Red River to Alexandria, Natchitoches, or Shreveport, and the military occupation of Northern Texas."

Banks had his own ideas about how Texas should be assaulted. To him the long, lightly defended Texas coast was an ideal target for an invasion. The possibility of a concerted attack on the Texas coast had been explored in the latter part of 1862, when a large Union force had easily captured the port city of Galveston. Although Union troops had been quickly forced out of the city by a well-conceived and executed Confederate assault, led by "Prince John" Magruder, the success of the original attack had shown that the forces in Texas could not defend the entire length of the state's coastline. Banks believed that a well-armed attack could knife into the state and allow him to establish a Union stronghold.[1]

Therefore in September, 1863, a large Union flotilla, including four gunboats and twenty-two troop carriers, steamed up the Sabine River to attack the Confederates at Fort Griffin. The southerners' position was an earthwork fort defended by 47 men under the command of Lieutenant Richard W. Dowling. Amazingly, the Union force was thrown back by the defenders, who maintained a persistent fire of one shell every two minutes. Meanwhile, missiles from the cannon aboard the Union ships bounced harmlessly off the earthen walls. The Union force was compelled to retreat, leaving two gunboats disabled and 350 men in the hands of the southerners. Texas remained Confederate.[2]

Even after his plan to invade at Sabine Pass failed, Banks remained opposed to a suggested invasion by way of the Red River. He decided that another strike along the coast would better serve his country. Troops were landed at the mouth of the Río Grande, and the defenders were routed. A Union beachhead had been established in Texas, but it consisted of only one town. Lincoln was unimpressed.[3]

While Banks was attempting to invade Texas along the coast, the president and his close advisers grew more adamant in their suggestions to the commander. Halleck wrote to Banks on January 4, 1864, that Major General William T. Sherman agreed "that the Red River is the shortest and best line of defense for Louisiana and Arkansas and as a base of operations against Texas."[4] Banks chaffed under this pressure, asserting that the Red River was a dangerous and difficult route for invasion, but Halleck persisted. Finally, in late January, Banks ceased his protests, writing to Halleck his agreement that the Red was the shortest and best line of assault. The reasons for his sudden change in attitude were simple. Sherman had offered to lend part of his force in Mississippi to the effort, Halleck seemed determined, and Lincoln had a propensity for removing commanders who were overly quarrelsome. Indeed, Banks had received his position in Louisiana because the former commander, Benjamin F. Butler, had lost the president's favor. Also, rumors persisted that huge supplies of cotton were stored along the Red River, enough to make a money-wise general wealthy.[5]

Once Banks was convinced, his only problem was carrying out the invasion. To coordinate the effort, Banks wrote on January 25 to Brigadier General Frederick Steele, commander of the Department of Arkansas, asking for aid. The same day he wrote Sherman, asking what assistance he could provide.

Halleck replied characteristically to Banks's agreement to a Red River approach that he had no intention of designing a campaign for Banks. He added that he was pleased to see the validity of his suggestions for an invasion up the Red River had finally been recognized. The general-in-chief also refused to appoint an over-all commander for the expedition.[6]

Sherman responded to Banks's missive by going to New Orleans in March. He was fresh from a slashing excursion across Mississippi, and he wanted to command the invasion up the Red. He found Banks prepared for the invasion and ready to lead the expedition personally. Inasmuch as Banks outranked him, Sherman promised to send him as many men as possible and left, grumbling that Banks was delaying the invasion to attend the inauguration of the new Union governor of Louisiana, Michael Hahn.[7]

General Steele's reply to Banks was as evasive as that from Halleck. He complained that elections were soon to be held in Arkansas and that his troops would be needed to oversee the balloting. In Mississippi, Sherman noted, "If we have to modify military plans for civil elections, we had better go home." Steele did suggest, however, that a mere feint by his forces toward Shreveport, the primary target of the invasion, might suffice. He was tired, undermanned, and overworked.[8]

Except for Sherman, Banks's colleagues seemed little concerned with his plight or with the success of the mission. Grant believed that all available Union forces should be utilized east of the Mississippi but wanted to aid Banks if possible. Early in March he was appointed general-in-chief of the army, replacing Halleck, and on March 15 he wired Steele, "Move your force in full cooperation with General N. P. Banks. A mere demonstration will not be sufficient."[9] Grant's reputation for brevity and straightforwardness was well deserved.

The last cog in the machinery for an invasion was in gear when Admiral David Porter promised his cooperation, declaring that he would ascend the Red River with "every ironclad vessel in the fleet." Banks was ready—at least materially—for

General Nathaniel Banks. Brave and ambitious, Banks was no match for the Confederate forces he encountered while leading the invasion of Texas and Louisiana. Courtesy of the National Archives.

the invasion of Texas. The Red River Campaign was about to begin. Almost fifty thousand men would be sent against Confederate defenders in northwestern Louisiana and east Texas.[10]

The massive Union land force would be under the command of Major General Banks. Yet Halleck's refusal to appoint an over-all commander—a decision that would plague the expedition—created a vacuum of authority and left the design and execution of the campaign to the commander of the Department of the Gulf. Although Banks could have chosen another man to lead the force in the field, the glories of a successful invasion of Texas—which he believed assured—lured him from the refinements and delights of the Crescent City; Nathaniel Banks was a man who believed himself destined for greater things—perhaps even the presidency.[11]

Nathaniel Prentiss Banks was born in Waltham, Massachusetts, in 1816. His formal education was cut short by his family's economic situation. Finding employment at the textile mill where his father worked as a superintendent, he received the nickname "Bobbin Boy of Massachusetts," which clung to him in later life. Despite his humble beginning, Banks was determined and ambitious, teaching himself Latin and Spanish as well as oratory and acting. He turned to law, passing the bar examinations in 1839. He decided to make politics his future. As a Democrat he was elected to the Massachusetts lower house in 1849 and to the national Congress in 1852. He was reelected to Congress in 1854 as a member of the Know-Nothing Party, beginning his conversion to Republicanism. In 1858 he was elected governor of his home state and retained that position until 1860, when he became president of the Illinois Central Railroad, succeeding George B. McClellan.

At the beginning of the Civil War, Banks was commissioned a major general of volunteers. His first service was in the Department of Annapolis, but he was soon transferred to the Department of the Shenandoah, where he received the dubious honor of facing Thomas ("Stonewall") Jackson. Despite Jackson's successes, Banks fought well. After facing Jackson, Banks commanded the defenses of Washington until his appointment as commander of the Department of the Gulf, where he took part in the siege of Vicksburg.[12]

As a soldier, Banks was more determined and confident than talented. At Vicksburg he had ordered direct assaults that had resulted in heavy losses, though his determination had aided in the success of the siege. Banks was one of the many political generals of the Civil War, appointed for his attitudes and inclinations rather than for military prowess. Ambitious to a fault, he eyed the presidential election of 1864 with relish, believing that his past services combined with a successful invasion of Texas would sweep him into the highest office in the land. Therefore he enthusiastically assumed command of the Red River Campaign. Throughout his life determination and hard work had sufficed, overcoming his deficiencies. As the invasion of Texas began, he had little doubt that the same formula would succeed again—and the Bobbin Boy would bask in the appreciation of his nation.[13]

Banks colleagues did not share his optimism. Sherman believed him incompetent to command a large-scale operation, noting that he was better at gala affairs or in political debates than at killing people. Sherman had little patience with citizen soldiers—especially those who commanded operations he wanted to lead. Steele, who would show his disrespect for Banks during the campaign, thought him excitable and unorganized. Only Grant had confidence in Banks, because of his determination at Vicksburg; determination was an attribute that Grant admired.[14]

Unfortunately for Nathaniel Banks, many Confederates, whose spirits had been grizzled and hardened by years of adversity, were waiting for his invasion on the Red River. They were the men who would teach Banks another attribute—humility.[15]

Since the failure of the Union flotilla at Sabine Pass, Confederate authorities in the trans-Mississippi West had waited for another assault on Texas. The attack was the direct concern of three men: Lieutenant General Edmund Kirby-Smith, commander of the Trans-Mississippi Department, headquartered at Shreveport; Major General Richard Taylor, commander of the District of West Louisiana, also centered at Shreveport; and Major General John Bankhead Magruder, commander of the District of Texas, whose headquarters wandered around the state with the commander. Kirby-Smith and Taylor were convinced that the Union invasion would come by way of the Red River; Magruder, kept busy—and agitated—by the landing that Banks had ordered at the mouth of the Río Grande, believed that the main Union column would strike there.[16]

Through the winter of 1863–64, Kirby-Smith and Taylor worried over the prospects of a Union invasion, believing that

General Edmund Kirby-Smith, director of the Confederacy's fortunes in the
trans-Mississippi theater of operations, disagreed with his subordinate,
Richard Taylor, over strategy, but he was wise enough to allow Taylor a free
hand in repulsing Union thrusts up the Red River. Courtesy the National
Archives.

the assault would come when the water level of the river rose to allow passage of gunboats and troop transports. Then news of Sherman's thrust into Mississippi arrived. The meaning of this development appeared clear: the next major Union operation would be east of the Mississippi. Officials in Mobile braced for an onslaught, and Kirby-Smith and Taylor relaxed—but only slightly. Magruder continued to eye the Union troops at Brownsville.[17]

Despite the appearance of Union intentions, the reality of Banks's presence in Louisiana bothered Taylor. He asked Kirby-Smith whether Banks could attack Texas without support from Sherman. The reply was equally baffling. Kirby-Smith wrote, "I still think that the enemy cannot be so infatuated as to occupy a large force in this department when every man should be employed east of the river, where the result of the campaign this summer must be decisive of our future."[18] Evidently Kirby-Smith agreed with Grant; Mobile seemed the logical target. Banks, however, was not in Louisiana without reason. Preparations had to be made for a Union invasion. Taylor was ordered to gather his forces, and Magruder was asked to move his troops from Texas to the Red. The first order was executed; Taylor marshaled his forces on the Red. Magruder was unable to comply with the command. Public officials in Texas considered "Prince John" an autocrat, and they opposed stripping Texas of its defenders. When Magruder attempted to march from Texas across the Sabine, a public outcry arose, and he was forced to remain in Texas with many of his troops. Still, the aid Taylor did receive from Texas would prove decisive.[19]

Richard Taylor had fewer than fifteen thousand men, while Banks had approximately twenty-five thousand. The situation looked grim for the Confederates, though they held one advantage; they were commanded by an experienced and talented warrior—Richard Taylor, the son of former President Zachary Taylor.[20]

Richard Taylor was born near Louisville, Kentucky, on his

Lieutenant General Richard Taylor, brilliant son of President Zachary Taylor, inherited much of his father's stubbornness. He prolonged the war by defeating the Union invasion up the Red River. Courtesy of the National Archives.

family's estate, "Springfields." His education ranged from private tutoring to studying at Edinburgh, Harvard, and Yale. In 1845 he graduated from Yale, and in 1848 he established his own estate, "Fashion," in Saint Charles Parish, Louisiana. Because of the influence of his father, Taylor was originally Whig, but his political inclination had changed toward the Democratic party during the 1850s, although he opposed secession. In 1861 he was elected a delegate to the secession convention in Charleston, where he was swayed by the emotions of the times and voted for secession. Appointed chairman for military and naval affairs at the convention, Taylor argued that the South should prepare itself for war, which he believed was inevitable. In July, 1861, he was appointed a colonel of the Ninth Louisiana Infantry, and in October he was made a brigadier general. Serving under Stonewall Jackson, Taylor demonstrated his courage and skill both in the Battle of Shenandoah Valley and the Battle of Seven Days. In July, 1862, he was sent to his home state as commander of the District of West Louisiana. There he enjoyed his command by constantly harassing the northerners in New Orleans with raids on their outposts and by seizing gunboats that ventured too far upriver. As a person, "Dick" Taylor was easy to respect but hard to like. He was stubborn, quick-tempered, and quixotic, and those characteristics, combined with boldness and skill, made him a valued commander. These same characteristics often earned him the spite and contempt of his fellow officers. Kirby-Smith, his immediate superior, found him difficult, argumentative, and, at times, antagonistic. For his part, Taylor thought the commander of the trans-Mississippi West was self-centered and bureaucratic, noting that "hydrocephalus at Shreveport [Kirby-Smith's headquarters] produced atrophy elsewhere."[21] Despite the personal differences between the two men, Taylor's ability to fight was beyond question.

The invasion began on March 12 and was a muddled affair from the start. Sherman had sent ten thousand troops from

Mississippi by transports under command of Brigadier General Andrew J. Smith. Admiral Porter's flotilla entered the Red River carrying these men. Two divisions under Smith's command were landed at Simmesport, a few miles up Atchafalaya River. From Simmesport, Smith marched northeast toward Fort De Russy, the first Confederate fortification on the Red. Meanwhile, Porter pushed his fleet upriver, coordinating his attack with Smith, thus allowing an assault on southern positions from land and water. Porter's fleet numbered fifteen ironclads and four tinclads, as well as several troop carriers. Banks and most of the Union force remained in New Orleans, waiting for the inauguration of Governor Hahn.

While commanding the Confederates in the area between Simmesport and Fort De Russy, Major John G. Walker received the distressing news that a massive Union column reportedly containing over fifteen thousand Yankees had been embarked at Simmesport. Walker, with less than four thousand effective soldiers, determined that the two-pronged Union attack made his position untenable. He must retreat. Although his estimate of the Union force at Simmesport was grossly inflated, Walker's position was insecure. Smith's two divisions numbered almost ten thousand, more than twice as many as Walker's force contained. Also, to remain between De Russy and Simmesport courted engulfment of the Confederate force. Should the Union gunboats pound the fort into submission, Walker's line of retreat would be endangered, perhaps lost. Thus Walker retreated to Bayou Du Lac, twenty miles west of Fort De Russy, where he was safe for the moment.[22]

Walker's retreat cleared the path to the back door of Fort De Russy for Smith's divisions. On March 13 scouts reported the retreat of the southerners to Smith, and the commander ordered his forces toward Marksville, a small town on the main road five miles southwest of Fort De Russy. On March 15 these troops reached the Confederate position and began preparations for a siege.[23]

While Smith's soldiers were enjoying a walk across the

Louisiana countryside, Admiral Porter's naval expedition was busy. To deter the Yankees, the Confederates placed several barricades in the Red. Almost two days were spent in breaching these obstacles; on March 15 the ironclads *Eastport* and *Neosho* broke through the barriers and proceeded to the Confederate fort, arriving at the same time as Smith's column.[24]

The battle was joined almost immediately. Smith's troops surrounded the fort, and Porter's gunboats shelled the southerners. Inside the walls three hundred Confederates waited for the inevitable. About six o'clock, two hours after the battle began, Brigadier General Joseph Mower personally led the Third Division into the structure. The defenders, outmanned and shellshocked, surrendered. Union losses were thirty-eight dead and wounded.[25]

Hoping to catch the Confederates at Alexandria, Porter sent his fastest gunboats ahead. They arrived in time to see the last Confederate steamer pass beyond the horizon. General Taylor had originally opposed Kirby-Smith's suggestion to construct Fort De Russy, and he had had little faith that it would effectively block a Union invasion. Realizing that an engagement with the invaders at Alexandria would almost surely end in defeat, Taylor moved his munitions and materiel upriver to Natchitoches. The quickness of the invasion caught the Confederates before they could mass. Taylor's only choice was to retreat until he could unify his command and ready a concerted defense.[26]

To achieve this goal, Taylor moved to Bayou Boeuf, twenty miles southwest of Alexandria. There he joined the commands of Camille Armand Jules Marie, Prince de Polignac, and Brigadier General Alfred Mouton. Having collected almost seven thousand men, Taylor began his retreat toward Natchitoches, watching the Union forces and waiting for the right moment and place to make his stand.[27]

While Taylor was making his orderly retreat, Porter moved part of his force from Fort De Russy to Alexandria to assume control of the abandoned town, seizing three cannon that the

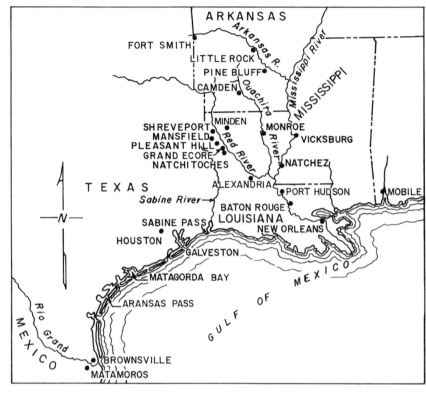

The area of Civil War operations along the Red River.

Confederates had inadvertently left behind. On March 20, Banks arrived with the forward elements of his fifteen thousand troops. The rest of his men were strung along the roads between New Orleans and Alexandria. The Confederate position appeared to be worsening. A concerted effort upriver by Banks's troops and Porter's gunboat would surely carry any Confederate defenders. Several problems loomed in the background. General Grant, who had become commanding general of the army, was determined that the troops whom Sherman had lent to Banks should be returned as soon as possible. On March 26 he wrote to Banks that, if it appeared by mid-April that Shreveport would not be taken by the end of that month, Smith's two divisions were to be returned to Sherman immediately. Grant still believed that the war would be won in the East. In addition to Grant's deadline, Banks was troubled by incomplete knowledge of the area. Was there a road along the Red that would allow his troops to remain near Porter's fleet? What was the best line of advance? Banks, still confident of victory, pondered these problems at Alexandria.[28]

While Banks mulled over his problems concerning the river, Taylor had others of his own to face. One of his primary problems was the insufficient number of cavalry in his command. He had only the cavalry of Colonel William G. Vincent, numbering 250 men. On March 19, Taylor, attempting to obtain information about the movements of Union forces, sent Vincent's force toward Bayou Rapides, between Boeuf and Alexandria. After jousting with the forward portion of the Union force, on March 21, Vincent settled his men near a place called Henderson's Hill. Here the sleeping Confederates were surrounded and captured by a large Union force under the command of General Mower. Taylor suddenly had lost what little cavalry he had. He could only wait for more horsemen to arrive from Texas, if indeed any were coming.[29]

The matter of reinforcements from Texas was another problem that bothered Taylor. Brigadier General Tom Green's force of Texans was supposed to be headed for Louisiana, but they had not arrived. Taylor needed them badly. If Banks decided to push up the river before the reinforcements arrived, Taylor might be forced to retreat into east Texas—or worse, be forced to fight the larger Union force without reinforcements.[30]

By March 25 the last portion of Banks's force had slogged into Alexandria. Heavy rains and muddy roads had slowed the column and delayed its arrival. Finally the entire invasion force was ready for action, and it was an impressive—almost overwhelming—collection of men and equipment. Banks had more than thirty thousand men, and Porter had twenty-one gunboats and more than forty troop transports. The combined number of cannon was three hundred: 210 were mounted on the boats, and 90 were with the infantry. Little wonder that Banks was confident.[31]

Banks did not believe that Taylor would fight, predicting that the Confederates would retreat to Shreveport. Thus the decision about which road Banks's infantry and cavalry would take seemed unimportant. The troops were just going to walk and ride to Natchitoches and then to Shreveport.

The matter of getting Porter's fleet past the rapids in the Red was another matter.[32] The Red rose each year in December or January, swollen by winter rains. In 1864 the rise was late, beginning in February, and it was small. Doubtless the cause was insufficient rainfall on the upper watershed of the river; to the Union navy, however, it must have seemed sheer orneriness. Since the gunboats had entered the mouth of the Red, snags, sandbars, and floating rafts of timber had hampered progress, and now the river refused to rise.[33]

Low water made the rapids a formidable barrier to Porter's ironclads. The admiral advised Banks that the big boats would have to be left behind at Alexandria; the lighter tinclad boats could navigate the rapids without difficulty. Banks replied that he needed all of Porter's fleet to ensure the success of the mission, and would the admiral please get his boats upriver.[34]

Porter agreed but remained uncertain of the advisability of taking his force above the rapids, wondering how he would get

134

them down again if the water level did not rise. He readied his boats for the dash over the rapids, planning to send his largest and deepest boat, the *Eastport*, over the shallows first. Porter evidently had decided that if the *Eastport* could navigate the rapids all of his fleet could do likewise, and if the boat ran aground the river would be blocked, preventing the passage of the rest of the fleet. Either way Porter would be satisfied.[35]

As expected, the *Eastport* jammed in the rapids, but the river finally rose enough for the great engine of war to pass. Porter then sent twelve more of his craft upriver. Soon the *Eastport, Chillicothe, Carondelet, Louisville, Mound City, Pittsburgh, Osage, Ozark, Neosho, Fort Hindman, Cricket, Juliet,* and *Lexington* steamed up over the rapids.

Meanwhile, Banks's land force had departed for Natchitoches under the command of Major General William B. Franklin. Andrew J. Smith's men were transported upstream by boat.[36] By April 3 all parties had reached Natchitoches, but the southerners had again retreated before the Union forces could make contact. While Porter's sailors seized tons of cotton as prizes of war, Banks sailed up the Red to Grand Écore, four miles above Natchitoches. The time had come for him to decide which road his troops would take. There was a road that followed the west bank of the Red, but Banks evidently did not know of its existence. Apparently he believed his choice was between the road that led to Minden, a village about twenty-five miles east of Shreveport, or the road that formed a rough semicircle between Grand Écore and Shreveport, passing through Pleasant Hill and Mansfield. Thinking that the route did not matter, Banks chose the latter.[37]

Banks returned to Natchitoches to review his troops. Surely a man such as Nathaniel Banks must have gloried in the knowledge that early heroes such as Louis Juchereau de St. Denis and Athanase de Mézières had been the masters of the town he now possessed.

On April 6 his troops began departing from Grand Écore, heading toward Pleasant Hill and their rendezvous with the enemy. Unknown to the troops or to Banks, the Confederates had arranged a welcome while the Union forces were parading in Natchitoches. Taylor had retreated to Mansfield, fretting over the delay of aid from Texas. There on April 5 he was gratified by the arrival of five thousand cavalrymen from Texas under the command of "Fighting Tom" Green, who recently had been recommended for promotion to major general. The appearance of Green, a veteran of the Texas Revolution and the Mexican War, and a fearless and respected commander, eased Taylor's worries a little. Also, General Kirby-Smith ordered detachments from Major General Sterling Price's command in Arkansas to move south to aid in the conflict. With the addition of these men Taylor had almost fifteen thousand troops.[38]

He was outnumbered almost two to one, but Taylor realized that the odds were not going to improve. During the time he had spent with Stonewall Jackson in the Shenandoah Valley, Taylor had learned the advantages of speed from the master of alacrity. Despite Kirby-Smith's vacillation between a fight in Louisiana and a retreat into east Texas, Taylor decided to deploy his forces. Unless his commanding general ordered him out of Louisiana, he was through retreating. He had chafed during the early retreat before Banks's invading army, for he thought little of Yankees in general and even less of Major General Nathaniel Banks.[39]

Luckily for the South, Kirby-Smith continued to be uncertain about the correct course he should follow and allowed Taylor to remain to Louisiana. Taylor was determined to fight before the enemy reached Mansfield. He knew that his force was outnumbered. He realized that he had to select a battlesite that would allow him to concentrate his forces. The area between Pleasant Hill and Mansfield was excellent because the northerners would be confined to one road. Past Mansfield, three roads led to Shreveport, and Taylor could not concentrate his forces on all three. Thus he applied simple logic, which Banks apparently missed. Taylor set about teaching the Bobbin Boy a lesson in military strategy.[40]

On April 8, Taylor began his preparations to defend Mansfield, ordering the infantry under Price from its camp at Keatchie to Mansfield. The commands of Generals Mouton and Walker were ordered to position themselves south of the town. By the ninth Taylor had almost nine thousand men on the road leading to Mansfield. Banks, who had expressed his worry that the enemy would never stop and fight, would have his battle.[41]

The forward elements of the Union column had reached Pleasant Hill on April 7, and that afternoon the mounted infantry of Brigadier General Albert Lee had clashed with a detachment of Green's Texans, getting their first taste of combat—a decidedly unpleasant taste. Green's men, unlike the Confederates whom the northerner had met before during the campaign, did not fall back. Instead they performed their commander's favorite maneuver—a charge. Although the Texans were beaten back with the aid of reserves, the skirmish was a demonstration of what would follow.[42]

The next morning Lee's column pushed ahead, meeting resistance but progressing. About noon the column reached a large clearing, extending almost a thousand yards before the advancing soldiers. In the midst of the space was an abrupt rise. Atop it the northerners saw a line of Confederates. Although their position appeared strong, the southerners were driven back.[43]

Lee sent skirmishers ahead to locate the bulk of the Confederate force. They found Walker's division—ready for battle. Lee had seen enough; he had no desire to lead his men into a hornet's nest. After convincing Banks that he would be unwise to charge into the bristling Confederate position, Lee stationed his men before the enemy and waited. It was four o'clock, and the air was heavy with tension, excitement, and fear. The two armies waited, one sick of retreats and running, the other wondering what had happened to Banks's boast that he would be in Shreveport by April 10.[44]

Banks wanted to bring up more infantry. He evidently realized that he had unwittingly allowed Taylor to concentrate his forces in front of the long stretch of Union soldiers. But there was little he could do. Behind Lee's mounted cavalry was the baggage train, consisting of hundreds of wagons and stretching for miles. After these wagons came Franklin's infantry. Banks had the superior force in the area, but he could not bring the full extent of his power into action. Wagons blocked the road, and it would take time to bring Franklin's infantry forward. Banks's only hope was that Taylor would not assume the offensive.[45]

Either Dick Taylor realized Banks's predicament or else he simply ran out of patience and ordered General Mouton to attack. The Louisiana contingent swept down on the right flank of the enemy.[46] Brigadier General T. E. G. Ransom's flank repulsed the first charge for the North, but the fighting continued. After Mouton's forces had engaged the enemy, Walker unleashed his eager Texans on the northerners' left flank. Like their fathers who fought at San Jacinto and in Mexico City, the Texans charged, screaming their demonic exhortations, spurring their compatriots to higher accomplishments, and tingling the spines of many untested Yankees. Soon the left flank of the defenders collapsed. Whole regiments were annihilated or captured. General Ransom quickly ordered a retreat.[47]

Falling back, the Union troops found some small support in a line of reinforcements that General Franklin had hurriedly formed near the edge of the clearing. Realizing the danger, Franklin had led a division of his infantry to the front, and for a time the line held. But the southerners kept coming, charging and shouting, shooting and stabbing. Minié balls sang their siren songs of death, luring some men to destruction and pushing others to cowardice. Friends and brothers were suddenly only cold and leaden memories lying on the ground—

and still the wild men came. Suddenly, as if some long-angered god had passed among the men, whispering the prophecy of impending doom, panic raced through the Union ranks. Men threw down their weapons and fled, burning with fear and hearing only the din in their own minds. No longer was there a battle, but a rout, a debacle, a tragedy.[48]

Fortunately, Franklin not only brought reinforcements but also saw that his position would not stand. Therefore he ordered Brigadier General William H. Emory to advance with a division of the 19th Corps to a favorable location in the rear and form another line. Emory placed his men in a small streambed near Pleasant Grove and waited. The men of his division were greeted by the fleeing soldiers, who warned that demons and devils were following. The Confederates soon appeared.[49] Unfettered emotions seemed to be contagious. The hysteria that had broken and scattered Banks's army spread to Taylor's and was translated into elation. When the northerners had fled, the Confederates pursued in disorganized bunches. Arriving at Emory's position, they attacked piecemeal and were repulsed. The defenders were finally driven from the stream, but the southerners could not break the resistance. Darkness soon ended the madness for a time. The sounds of the living then were replaced by the wails of men about to die. It had been a day that many men would remember with pride, while others would feel only shame, but the night was one that men on both sides would spend a lifetime trying to forget.[50]

More than 2,000 Union soldiers were dead, wounded, or missing. Thousands of small arms, eighteen cannon, and more than 150 wagons and their teams had been lost to the southerners. Taylor had extracted a heavy fee from Banks for a lesson in logic. Fewer than 1,000 Confederates were dead or wounded. Considering that Banks had deployed more than 12,000 men in the battle, whereas Taylor had had only 8,800 troops, the results were remarkable.[51]

Regardless of the battle, Banks was still confident. Emory's

139

line had held, and Banks was still going to Shreveport. For a time he considered bringing Smith's 16th Corps to the line Emory had established, but his subordinates convinced him that the move would be unwise. The 13th Corps, which had taken the brunt of the attack, was a shambles. No force on earth would persuade the men who had fled in panic to stand and fight. Finally Banks decided to regroup his forces at Pleasant Hill, fifteen miles southeast of Mansfield. There Smith's troops were deployed on the rise that gave the place its name. It was Taylor's move.[52]

Seeing that Banks had retreated to Pleasant Hill, Taylor led his force forward. He had been joined by the forces sent from Price under the command of Brigadier General Thomas J. Churchill. Surveying the situation, he devised his battle plan, a masterful but complex scheme. Churchill was to march to the road leading from the Sabine River toward Pleasant Hill, approaching the Union troops from the southeast. This move was expected to crush the enemy's left flank. Meanwhile, Walker was to lead his Texans down the road from Mansfield, attacking the middle of the Union position. When these movements had disorganized the defenders, Brigadier General Hamilton P. Bee would descend from Walker's left with his mounted Texans. Polignac, in command of the slain Mouton's division, was held in reserve on the road to Mansfield.[53]

At five o'clock the battle began. Churchill swept in from the defenders' left, and Walker pushed forward after hearing the sounds of battle. The fight went as planned. Tom Green, however, thinking that the northerners had been put to flight, ordered Bee to commence his assault. The Texans rode into a wicked cross fire that repulsed their attack and caused them to take heavy losses. Walker had received a similar greeting. Churchill's force was making headway, rolling up the left flank. Taylor, seeing that Bee and Walker had been stymied, ordered Polignac into the fray. The center of the Union line was carried, and the Confederates threatened to surround the right flank of the enemy commanded by Brigadier General William Dwight. The Union forces appeared in danger of suffering their second overwhelming defeat in as many days.[54]

Just as the situation seemed hopeless, the 58th Illinois, which had been held in reserve, attacked Churchill and stopped his progress. Andrew Smith, commanding on the left flank, ordered his troops to charge. The right flank of the Confederates was crushed. The attack had been repulsed. Taylor's only choice was to retreat. As the Confederates fell back, it was their turn to feel panic, and the battle ended.[55]

Banks thus had won a victory—and was still determined to press his invasion to Shreveport. But his commanders knew better. The Union forces had been lucky not to be overwhelmed. The men were tired and discouraged, and they had lost faith in Banks. The commander was finally persuaded to withdraw and break off the invasion. Banks ordered his force to retreat to Grand Écore, where Porter's boats would transport them downriver.[56]

While Taylor's force was pushing the northerners back from Mansfield, Admiral Porter had steamed part of his force up the Red, reaching Springfield Landing, thirty miles from Shreveport. Banks had promised to meet him there to reunite the land and naval arms of the expedition for the final assault on Shreveport. Leaving Grand Écore, Porter had been unable to take his entire fleet upriver. The Red had not freshened yet, and the water level remained too low for some of his craft. Only six of the gunboats, the admiral's flagship, the *Osage*, and the *Cricket*, the *Neosho*, the *Fort Hindman*, the *Lexington*, and the *Chillicothe*, were able to navigate the shallow waters above Grand Écore. They were accompanied by twenty troop carriers. To protect the boats, part of the 16th Corps under the command of Brigadier Thomas Kilby Smith had remained with the fleet.[57]

. The voyage upriver had been uneventful except for frequent stops to free boats that had run aground. When Porter reached Springfield Landing on April 10, he found the channel blocked by the wreckage of the *New Falls City*, a large steamer that the Confederates had scuttled to slow the Union fleet. Waiting at the rendezvous point, Porter was informed of the action at Mansfield and Pleasant Hill and of the decision to retreat.[58]

Porter was in a dangerous position. The confidence of the invaders had led them to plunge headlong into the heart of enemy country. Porter, like Banks, was brash and confident in the abilities of his fleet. Given to bold statements, he once boasted that his boats could go anywhere "the sand was damp."[59] Such boldness and confidence had brought him to Springfield Landing.[60]

While Banks's troops had been nearby, available to help defend the fleet, there was little danger to the boats. The Confederate naval forces on the Red were nil, and with the infantry, cavalry, and artillery of Banks's force at hand the armada was truly invincible. Banks's decision to send his troops on the inland route through Mansfield had changed the situation drastically, and the defeat of the northerners and subsequent withdrawal to Grand Écore left Porter's fleet open to assault from land. If the Confederates made a concerted attack on the fleet, the results probably would be unfavorable for the Union. Indeed, the addition of several gunboats to the Confederate navy would change Union fortunes in the Mississippi and Gulf region. Porter consequently ordered a hasty retreat downriver, having been advised that Banks would meet him at Grand Écore.[61]

Regardless of Admiral Porter's wishes, the flotilla's speed was limited by shallow water. Boats continually ran aground, and the officers knew that a boat stuck on the mud too long was courting attack by Confederates. Captain Thomas Selfridge, who commanded the *Osage*, found his craft unmanageable. On April 12 the transport *Black Hawk* was lashed to the starboard of the *Osage* to aid in navigation, but about two o'clock that afternoon it ran aground near Blair's Landing, forty-five river miles above Grand Écore.[62]

Meanwhile, many of Taylor's men had been recalled from the area to help repulse a Union column approaching Shreveport from Arkansas under the command of General Steele. Tom Green's cavalry was left to watch the retreat of the northerners.[63]

On the day the *Osage* ran aground at Blair's Landing, Green was notified of the event and immediately led his men to the scene. They arrived to find that the *Osage* had freed itself and had been joined by the gunboat *Lexington*. Green stationed his artillery near the banks of the river and prepared to attack. Captain Selfridge was informed of the presence of Confederates and ordered the *Lexington* to open fire. Green's Texans replied with their muskets, leading Selfridge to note later that "everything that was made of wood on the *Osage* and *Black Hawk* was pierced with bullets."[64] Green, relying on his standard tactic, ordered his forces to charge. The assault was repulsed by fire from the gunboats; Green was as usual in the midst of the action and was struck in the forehead by a cannon shell from the *Osage*, which killed him instantly.[65] With their commander dead and prospects of success few, the Confederates withdrew. Porter's fleet continued downriver to Grand Écore, bouncing and scraping all the way. The arrival of the boats greatly relieved Banks and his soldiers. Some had speculated that when the boats appeared they would be flying the Stars and Bars of the Confederacy. The joining of forces did not, however, end the problems facing Banks and Porter.[66]

At Grand Écore, Banks received orders from Sherman, demanding the return of Smith's corps. That would, in Banks's estimation, leave the Union forces grossly undermanned; he believed that Taylor had at least twenty-five thousand troops. Banks replied to Sherman that he could not comply; Smith's forces were needed on the Red. Banks realized, however, that Sherman would ask again, probably with Grant's support. His time was running out, and Porter's difficulties with the river were creating dangerous delays.[67]

The Red was still playing havoc with the admiral's fleet. The chute at Grand Écore effectively blocked the passage of several of the larger boats, and on April 14 the *Eastport*, having safely navigated the shallows, struck a torpedo and sank to the muddy bottom. The admiral needed time to get his fleet downriver, but time was a commodity that was dear to Banks.[68]

Not only was Sherman asking for his troops, but Banks felt that Taylor doubtless was nearby, laying plans. Banks wanted to return to Alexandria as soon as possible. Porter feared that the army would depart, leaving his stranded boats at the mercy of the southerners, but Banks promised to remain until the fleet was able to descend the river.[69]

Evidently Banks had learned from the lesson Taylor had taught him at Mansfield. Realizing that his enemy probably would attempt to block his retreat, on April 19 he dispatched General Smith downriver to prevent such an occurrence. Smith departed on April 21, the same day that Porter's boats were taken over the chute and the *Eastport* was raised from the bottom. The retreat from Grand Écore began.[70]

By the morning of the twenty-third the fleet and the army had evacuated Grand Écore, leaving the town in flames. Moving to Natchitoches, the army followed the course of the Cane River, an ancient bed of the Red that had long been forsaken by the waters of that river. Thirty miles downstream the Cane rejoined the Red, where a great island was formed in the area between the two rivers. Banks learned that Taylor's forces were headed for Monett's Ferry, the main crossing on the Cane, which the Union army had to use. Attempting to avoid the trap, Banks pushed his army relentlessly.[71]

For his part Taylor was aching from the destruction that the Union army had brought to his state. Everywhere houses and barns had been burned, livestock killed, and fields leveled. He wanted revenge. Thus with only five thousand men he attempted to surround Banks's force of twenty thousand.[72]

Arriving at Monett's Ferry first, the Confederates deployed. Their plan was simple. Major General John A. Wharton, who had recently arrived from Texas with a small brigade of cav-

144

alry, was to harass the Union column from the rear. Polignac's division was stationed near Cloutierville, a small town northwest of Monett's Ferry, and Hamilton Bee's force was placed at the crossing. He was ordered to hold his position at all costs because it was crucial in preventing the northerners from escaping.[73]

The plan was good, but after the Union assault began on the twenty-third, Bee mistakenly thought that the center of the Confederate position had been overwhelmed. In reality the Union charge had been repulsed, but Bee withdrew, assuming the battle was lost, and opened the road to Alexandria. Taylor was livid and removed Bee from his command. Nonetheless, the damage had been done. Banks was free to enter Alexandria.[74]

Admiral Porter was not faring as well as Banks. On April 26 the *Eastport* ran hard aground near the small town of Montgomery. All efforts to free the craft failed, and Porter reluctantly ordered the boat destroyed. The descent downriver then continued. Five miles above the mouth of the Cane the fleet came under heavy fire from the Confederate artillery. Two transports, the *Champion No. 3* and the *Champion No. 5*, were lost. Tragically, the former's boiler was struck by a shell and exploded, killing more than 150 blacks who had been picked up by the northerners. And the ironclads *Cricket*, *Juliet*, and *Fort Hindman* were severely damaged, with heavy losses among their crews.[75]

On April 28 all the boats had been run past the Confederate gunners and were collected at Alexandria. Matters were not much better there. Commanding General Grant was making growling noises in Banks's direction about the prompt return of Sherman's troops. Grant wanted Smith's corps east of the Mississippi. Banks wanted to comply, but Porter's boats were in trouble again—serious trouble.[76]

The rapids at Alexandria, the same ones that had worried Porter a month earlier, had the fleet trapped. The Red still had not risen, and twelve gunboats were above the rapids. If

Banks took his army downriver before the boats were rescued, the backbone of the fleet would be lost. The boats would have to be scuttled to prevent their capture by Confederates. Porter's career was on the verge of ruin. Admirals, no matter what their past accomplishments, did not lose twelve gunboats and retain Lincoln's favor. Porter, for once at a loss for an answer, or even a boast, asked for suggestions.[77]

Lieutenant Colonel Joseph Bailey, chief engineer for the 19th Corps, approached Porter and proposed building a dam across the river below the rapids. It would raise the water level on the rapids and allow the boats to cross. Once the boats were over the rapids, the dam could be removed, and the fleet could continue. It was a good plan. The only question was the building of the dam. Below the rapids the river was almost three hundred feet wide, and the current was nearly ten miles an hour. Although Porter was unconvinced, the project was approved.[78]

The soldiers worked feverishly. Houses were demolished, and their timbers were used in the dam. Great trees were felled and added to the project. Finally, only a twenty-foot space separated the two wings of the dam. Two barges filled this hole. On May 8, the *Neosho*, the *Fort Hindman*, and the *Osage* crossed the rapids, but, for reasons unknown, the rest of the fleet remained. The soldiers, who had constructed the dam while the navy watched, suggested that the pilots of the boats had gone to sleep. Perhaps they were right.[79]

Whatever the reasons, the boats remained above the rapids that day, and on the morning of the ninth they again were trapped. The pressure of the water on the barges in the middle of the dam carried them away during the night. Only the *Lexington*, which Porter ordered to shoot the rapids as the dams disintegrated, was rescued. Bouncing on the river bottom, the *Lexington* pushed over the rapids and through the hole in the dam before the water disappeared. Eight boats remained above the rapids.[80]

146

Banks, who had watched the fleet's activity with interest, growled that he needed to get his army downriver. Grant was growing more adamant in his demands for the troops to be returned to Sherman, and the Confederates were still lurking in the woods. Bailey went back to work, building wing dams at the head of the rapids to concentrate the flow of the water. By the tenth the wing dams were completed, but the water was still too shallow. Another army engineer, Lieutenant Colonel U. B. Pearsall, suggested that a "bracket dam" would slow the current and back water sufficiently to allow the boats to pass. To Porter's relief this plan worked, and the boats were saved. With the final obstacle overcome, Porter led his fleet to the Mississippi, and Banks followed suit. By May 15 the Union forces had retreated below the Atchafalaya. The Red River Campaign was over.

Banks and Porter had accomplished their retreat none too soon. Steele's invasion from Arkansas had been repulsed by the end of April, and during the first week in May, Churchill's and Walker's forces were returned to Taylor. Fortunately for the northerners, just as Taylor reunited his forces and readied an assault, the invaders floated and marched down the Red.[81]

Several factors had combined to cause the failure of the Union invasion of northwest Louisiana and east Texas. Taylor's talents and his troops' dedication had helped, as had the Red River's refusal to rise. Banks's own mistakes, however, were basic to the failure. If he had not sent his troops on the inland road to Mansfield, Taylor's talents would have been untested, or at least used to defend the streets of Shreveport.

Despite the low water, Porter's flotilla eventually reached Springfield Landing. Had Banks marched his force along the river near the fleet, a combined water-and-land assault could have been launched, severely trying the defenders. Had the invaders approached Shreveport from Springfield Landing en masse, the Confederates would have been unable to mount a concerted defense against Steele's invasion from Arkansas.

The problem was not the plan proposed by Halleck to ascend the Red to Shreveport, but rather the execution of the plan by Nathaniel Banks.

At New Orleans, Banks received his reward for the campaign. There he was informed on May 7 that Major General Edward R. S. Canby had been named commander of the Military District of West Mississippi. Canby was given control of all military operations in the Departments of the Gulf and the Mississippi. Banks's political connections had prevented his complete removal from authority, for he remained at new Orleans. In name he still was commander of the Department of the Gulf; in reality he was only a figurehead. His military career was over, and his presidential aspirations were dead. He had found precious little glory on the Red River.[82]

9.

Peace and Prosperity

A year after Nathaniel Banks returned to New Orleans, the end came for the Confederate States of America. Such warriors as Robert E. Lee, Joseph Eggleston Johnston, Nathan Bedford Forrest, and Richard Taylor laid down their burdens, recognizing the inevitable. Their great cause was lost. In the trans-Mississippi West, Kirby-Smith and Magruder spoke empty phrases for a time of continuing the war, and then they slipped away to Mexico. Some, like Jo Shelby and his cavalrymen, mounted their horses and rode away, never acknowledging in defeat the mastery of those whom they had bested in war.

Soon Lincoln joined the hosts who had died during the tragedy, and something called "Radical Reconstruction" began. Slowly—sadly—the nation bound its wounds. As they had after the American Revolution, leaders, some good, some evil, set about forming a nation from the shambles. A new United States emerged, a different nation, altered forever by the upheaval of civil war. Some men hated it, others gloried in it, but most simply endured it. The Union had survived.

After the war ended, the country along the Red River was in ruins. Plantations and farms were gone, slaves were free, owners were dead. Cotton gins were charred frames, and steamboats were gutted hulls. But the people went to work, building and planting, mending and making. By 1870 the country was becoming productive again. Steamboats such as the *Arrow Line*, the *Belle Ida No. 2*, the *Big Horn*, the *Grand*

149

Era, the *Henry M. Shreve*, the *W. F. Curtis*, and the *Anne Everson* were ascending the river to Shreveport and Jefferson to take on cotton and carry it to New Orleans for sale. Even so, one problem remained: the raft.[1]

Work on the raft had ceased in the late 1850s because Congress refused to continue appropriating funds for what seemed a never-ending task. After the war ended, the issue was revived. In the winter of 1872, Lieutenant E. A. Woodruff of the Army Corps of Engineers was dispatched to Louisiana to survey the raft and estimate the cost of its removal. While in Louisiana, Woodruff received a letter from C. M. Hervey, a planter who owned a large tract of land on the Red near Washington, Arkansas. Hervey urged that work be commenced immediately to remove the raft, asserting that more than 200,000 acres of fertile bottomland could be reclaimed and that $150,000 could be saved each year in shipping fees, cotton prices, and insurance rates. He wrote in 1870 that high water and the growth of the raft had caused more than $400,000 to be wasted on sending shipments around the obstruction. Finally, Hervey noted that merely removing the raft would not suffice but that provisions had to be made to prevent a recurrence of the barrier.[2]

In his report Woodruff wrote:

That the removal of the raft and the prevention of its re-formation is desirable, hardly admits of discussion. The need of a cheap mode of transportation of the products of the upper river, the relief of valuable plantations made worthless by overflow, and the prevention of the ruin of more plantations above, are sufficient reasons to warrant extensive appropriations for these ends.[3]

He estimated the total cost of removing the raft in one year to be $116,000, with an additional cost of $98,000 to acquire the needed equipment. He suggested that annual appropriations ranging from $10,000 to $25,000 would be needed to prevent the reforming of the raft.[4]

Major General John B. Magruder. "Prince John" forced the Union forces off Galveston Island, compelling Nathaniel Banks to accept President Lincoln's plan to invade the Red River. Courtesy of the National Archives.

Congress was in a mood to comply, for the nation was demanding raw products to feed the industrial centers of the North. On June 10, 1872, it appropriated $150,000 to remove the raft. Little work was done in 1872, but considerable progress was made in 1873. In addition to using snag boats and winches to pull sections of the raft asunder, a new tool was utilized: nitroglycerin. The explosive was used to break up large sections of timbers that had become tightly packed. Such sections, called rafts by the workmen, had posed serious problems during previous attempts to free the Red because equipment was frequently damaged in attempts to pry the logs apart. Also the "nitro" was useful in breaking large timbers into small pieces that would float downriver. Captain C. W. Howell, the engineer in charge of the project, wrote in 1874:

In breaking the jams and cutting off snags, nitro-glycerine had been found indispensible, from 60 to 75 pounds being used in a day, generally in from 2 to 5 pound charges. For instance, the 31st [of October] was almost entirely spent in an unsuccessful attempt to remove a snag under water, which stopped all drift pulled [from floating downstream]: the last attempt for the day was made with a 7½-inch premium line led to the large steam-capstan of the Aid [one of the snag boats]. The capstan was 'stalled.' The next morning a 5-pound charge of nitro-glycerine removed the obstruction. [5]

In his report Howell also described the first application of the explosive in removing the raft:

Cans, containing from 10 to 20 pounds of nitro-glycerine, were sunk as near the bottom of the river as possible and exploded, with the effect of breaking the long logs and a general loosening of the mass in the immediate proximity. Small charges were also used in cutting long logs and stumps too far beneath the surface of the water to be operated on by other means. [6]

Although the work of removing the raft was slowed by low water, progress was made. Saw boats, designed, as the name implied, to cut timbers and brush, worked constantly, removing obstacles above the surface, while snag boats opened a channel through the raft, pulling stumps and timbers. In November, 1873, the channel finally was clear. Howell wrote:

> Operations . . . were continued until the evening of the 26th. The river at that time was rising rapidly, and at daylight on the 27th the remaining portion of the raft obstructing the channel went out, and Red River was relieved of a serious obstruction to its navigation. The most important of the work having been accomplished, preparation was at once made to return to the foot of the raft and improve the channel existing through the raft.[7]

The Red River raft had finally been conquered, but the job was not finished. The raft had to be prevented from forming again. Dams had to be built across bayous to prevent runoff from the main channel, and small rafts had to be removed. In 1875 the rapids at Alexandria were deepened. Thus another serious obstacle to navigation was eliminated. The next year the mouth of the river was deepened and widened. Work on the Red River by the Corps of Engineers continued until 1900, with yearly improvements. The channel was straightened at several bends of the river, and many "chutes," or shallows, were removed. Congressional appropriations from 1872 to 1900 for the improvement of the Red River, including the removal of the raft, amounted to $1,397,000. Total appropriations for improving the river, including surveys, were $2,403,377.50. Congress also appropriated $45,000 during the period 1886 to 1896 to improve Cypress Bayou.[8]

The effects of the raft's removal were as expected. Large amounts of land were reclaimed after the water drained downriver, costs of shipping products from the upper Red River valley were vastly reduced, and Shreveport became a busy port. Steamboats began ascending the river to Fulton, Arkansas, and then beyond the Great Bend. One negative result of the change was the demise of Jefferson, Texas, as a river port. Steamboats had been able to travel up Cypress Bayou from the Red to Jefferson before removal of the raft because the backwater had raised the water level of the bayou and of Caddo

Lake. When the raft was gone, the water level dropped, leaving Jefferson beyond the reach of steamers. Although work on Cypress Bayou by the Corps of Engineers between 1886 and 1896 revived the trade between Jefferson and the Red River, the town never attained its previous status as the second-largest port in Texas. Instead, Jefferson, which also was bypassed by the railroads, shrank to a small country town. Only the great antebellum plantation homes remained as symbols of Jefferson's past glories.[9]

In contrast to Jefferson's plight, other ports on the Red River were aided immeasurably by the removal of the raft. Railroads entered the area along the Red River during the 1870s, but traffic on the river continued to increase. In 1875 fourteen steamers were plying its course, making regular runs upriver. By 1881 twenty steamers were running regularly between Shreveport, the principal port on the Red, and New Orleans. The total carrying capacity of these boats was 64,630 tons. During the period September 1, 1800, to May 31, 1881, these boats carried downriver to New Orleans such varied items as beeswax, tallow, cotton, cottonseed and cottonseed oil, grain, hay, wool, and hides.

During this period 86,646 bales of cotton were carried to New Orleans from ports on the Red River. Because steamboat operators charged lower rates, the cargoes on boats out of Shreveport increased while the tonnage shipped by rail decreased. For the period mentioned, 21,193 bales of cotton were shipped by rail from Shreveport, whereas in the previous year 58,243 bales had been shipped. During the same period 37,474 bales of cotton were shipped from Shreveport by boat, whereas in the previous year only 14,181 bales had been carried downriver.[10]

During the following fiscal year, ending in June, 1882, almost 90,000 bales of cotton were delivered at New Orleans from ports on the Red, with 55,000 bales being shipped from Shreveport. Also, 45,000 sacks of cottonseed were shipped to New Orleans.[11]

While Shreveport was the center for trade on the Red, steamers were pushing farther upriver, reaching Fulton, Arkansas, and the mouth of the Kiamichi River. During the years 1880 and 1881 more than 14,000 bales of cotton were shipped to New Orleans from points above Shreveport.[12]

In the following fiscal year, 1883–84, traffic on the Red peaked. Twenty steamers were running from Shreveport to New Orleans, carrying 108,000 bales of cotton, 270,000 pounds of hides, 87,000 pounds of wool, 20,630 pounds of cottonseed cakes, 5,500 pounds of beeswax, and 18,000 pounds of tallow. In addition, 35,000,000 feet of lumber were shipped downriver from Shreveport. More than 160,000 bales of cotton were carried downstream. Partly as a result of the trade Shreveport grew from a town of fewer than 5,000 people in 1850 to 12,000 by 1884.[13]

During the fiscal year ending in June, 1886, shipping on the river decreased from that of 1884. The traffic, however, remained steady. Thirteen boats were engaged in the trade on the river, four on the upper Red above Shreveport, and nine on the lower river. The boats on the upper river ranged from one hundred to four hundred tons, whereas the boats trading below Shreveport ranged between two hundred and eight hundred tons. During 1886 the river was navigable to Kiamatia, Texas (near the Kiamichi River), for two months; to Fulton, Arkansas, for four months; and to Garland City, Arkansas (near the Louisiana-Arkansas border), for the entire year. During this period 11,000 bales of cotton and more than 48,000 sacks of cottonseed were shipped from the area above Shreveport. These figures demonstrate the effectiveness of the Corps of Engineers' work on the river.[14]

Also during 1886, more than 70,000 bales of cotton were shipped from Shreveport, as well as 125,000 pounds of hides and 120,000 barrel staves. The steamers made 108 trips between New Orleans and Shreveport, taking an estimated $2,500,000 worth of goods upriver.[15]

By 1890 competition from railroads had cut severely into

155

the riverboat traffic. Only eight boats were working between Shreveport and New Orleans, while two were engaged in the trade between Shreveport and Alexandria.[16] The Corps of Engineers reported:

> Red River is crossed by the St. Louis, Iron Mountain and Southern Railway at Fulton, Ark., and by the St. Louis, Arkansas, and Texas Railway (Cotton Belt Route) at Garland, Ark., and by the Vicksburg, Shreveport, and Pacific Railroad and a branch of the "Cotton Belt Route" at Shreveport. Two companies have applied for charters for bridges at Alexandria. The Texas, Pacific Railway, running nearly parallel to the river touches at Alexandrdia, Shreveport, and other points, and the Morgan's Louisiana, and Texas Railroad (Southern Pacific) has a branch running to Alexandria. All these lines divert a large percentage of the commerce.[17]

The figures for fiscal years 1888–89 and 1889–90 support this assertion. Whereas the trade in cotton transported by water for the former year had been 12,368 bales, it decreased in the latter to 8,897.[18]

Despite the decline, the work of the corps revived trade between Jefferson and Shreveport. During the year ending in June, 1890, two boats, the *New Haven* and the *Friendly*, made thirty-three round trips between these ports, carrying goods valued at $304,325. The railroads, however, which had bypassed Jefferson because of the town's failure to grant the roads large land concessions, realized the value of building feeder lines into the area. By 1890 a branch of the Texas and Pacific Railroad had reached Jefferson, as had a branch of the Missouri, Kansas, and Texas Railroad. These lines decreased public demand for steamboat traffic to the town.[19]

By 1894 only seven steamers were trading regularly between Shreveport and New Orleans, although the river was open to navigation the entire year. Several small boats were engaged in local trade on the river, and five boats were trading between several ports on the lower river, such as Index, Panola, and New Orleans. Only one steamer, the *Rose Bland*, plied be-

156

tween Shreveport and Jefferson, although the route between the ports was open seven months of the year.[20]

Shipments from Shreveport increased in 1890 to 19,218 bales of cotton but continually declined thereafter. Shipments for the following years were 10,567 bales for fiscal year 1891–92, 14,751 for 1892–93, and 9,246 for 1893–94. Conversely, shipments by rail were markedly greater. For the four railroads carrying goods from Shreveport—the Texas and Pacific; the Vicksburg, Shreveport, and Pacific; the Houston and Shreveport; and the St. Louis, Southwestern—the total number of cotton bales was 99,436 in fiscal year 1891–92, 58,220 in 1892–93, and 66,811 in 1893–94.[21]

The impact of the railroads was also felt on the upper river. The river remained open to navigation from July to August and from November to May, but only three steamers, the *C. R. Cummings*, the *Gamma*, and the *Florence*, engaged in trade in 1897. These carried 38,826 tons of goods on the river. The work of the Corps of Engineers had extended highwater navigation to Denison, Texas; the river was paralleled by a branch of the Texas and Pacific Railway from Fulton, Arkansas, to the mouth of the Kiamichi River. A branch of the St. Louis and San Francisco Railway crossed the river at Arthur, north of Paris, Texas, and a branch of the St. Louis, Iron Mountain, and Southern Railway crossed at Fulton, Arkansas. Competition for trade in the area was fierce.[22]

By 1900 only six steamers, the *Sunrise*, the *Valley Queen*, the *Electra*, the *W. T. Scovell*, the *Hallette*, and the *Gem*, were trading between Shreveport and New Orleans. The total amount of goods shipped from Shreveport increased slightly between the years 1895 and 1900, but the era of steamboating on the Red River obviously was ending.[23]

The report of the chief of engineers for 1909 noted the declining trade on the Red River:

Notwithstanding the facilities for quick transportation afforded by railways, the commerce of Red River until recent years has con-

157

sisted of large shipments of cotton, cotton seed and its products, lumber, staves, timber, etc., with heavy return freights of general merchandise and plantation supplies.

The commerce and navigation reported for eighteen years showed great variations, due to changing crop conditions, occasional periods of extraordinary low water during the busy season, and other causes, ranging in quantity from 66,376 to 279,946 tons per annum, with estimated values of from $1,506,500 to $9,185,000. The average for the eighteen years was 123,244 tons, valued at $4,359,900. . . .

In 1908, however, there was a marked decline of navigation above the mouth of Black River and the commerce reported in that stretch only amounted to 36,288 tons, valued at $198,240.[24]

Although steamers occasionally ascended the Red River to take on cargoes of cotton, the days of black smoke, "waiting on the levee," and steam whistles were soon gone forever, replaced by the chugging and wheezing of iron horses. Soon the murky, changeable waters of the Red as a highway for commerce were replaced by gleaming rivers of steel.

10.

Border War in the Courts

From the mouth of the Kiamichi River to its confluence with the Mississippi, the Red River has been surveyed, widened, deepened, navigated, changed—"improved" said the Corps of Engineers. Until 1860 geographic knowledge of the river west of the 98th meridian had been slight. Randolph Marcy's expedition in 1852 had discovered that the river rose in two forks rather than one, and a survey in 1857 by Majors A. H. Jones and H. M. C. Brown to determine the extent of the lands of the Choctaw and Chickasaw Indians had established the point where the 100th meridian crossed the South Fork, or Prairie Dog Town Fork, of the Red. The exact limits of the state of Texas and the Indian Territory had yet to be determined.[1]

The northern boundary of Texas, as stated in the Adams-Onís Treaty of 1819, was a line following "the course of the Rio-Roxo [Red River] Westward to the degree of Longitude, 100 West from London and west from Washington . . . . as laid down in Melishe's [sic] Map of the United States, published at Philadelphia, improved to the first of January 1818."[2] Problems over this boundary arose because the Melish map showed only one fork of the Red River. The existence of two forks of the river, discovered by Marcy, opened the question of which fork the Melish map had indicated. Inasmuch as the area between the confluence of the two forks and the 100th meridian consisted of more than 50,000 acres of land, the designation of the proper fork to be the boundary was significant.

Jones's and Brown's designation of the South Fork of the

river as the boundary of the Indian Territory might have settled the dispute, giving the area to the United States. By the
agreement that brought Texas into the Union in 1845, however, that state was granted the right to participate in the settlement of its boundaries. Exercising this right, Texas opposed
the designation of the South Fork as the principal branch of
the Red.[3]

In 1860 a joint commission composed of members appointed
by the United States and Texas was formed to settle the problem. Governor Sam Houston of Texas was informed that the
head of the delegation from the United States, John C. Clark,
intended to use the boundary designated by Jones and Brown
as a starting point for the survey. Houston protested that
surely the North Fork was the one indicated by the Melish
map, for Marcy had marked the headwaters of the North Fork
with a bottle that seemed to indicate that he believed it to be
the main channel. Moreover, the Melish map indicated that
the "Rio-Roxo" flowed near a range of mountains. Houston
noted that the North Fork passed near the Wichita Mountains
while the South Fork did not flow near any mountain range.
Therefore, Houston asserted, the boundary should follow the
North Fork.[4]

The work of the joint commissions proved futile. The Texas
leader, William H. Russell, considered the two delegations
separate entities and demonstrated considerable hostility toward the members of the American delegation. Little progress
was made, and the boundary survey ended without agreement
on which fork of the Red was the main branch.[5]

While the boundary commissioners were feuding, on February 8, 1860, officials in Texas decided to take the initiative,
designating the disputed territory Greer County, Texas. The
coming of the Civil War delayed the organization of this
county until 1868, when it was attached to nearby Montague
County for administrative purposes. In 1879 the United States
Congress created the Northern Judicial District of Texas,

placing Greer County under the jurisdiction of the courts of Texas. Believing that Texas would eventually win the dispute over the area, state officials assumed ownership of the public lands in the region, and in 1881 began distributing allotments in the county to veterans of the Texas Revolution.[6]

Also in 1881, Congressman Olin Welborn of Texas introduced a bill in the House of Representatives designating the North Fork of the Red River as the boundary of Texas. Although the bill died in committee, the next year Senator Samuel B. Maxey of Texas introduced a bill calling for the creation of a joint boundary commission to settle the dispute and award the territory to his state. That bill also died. Most of the legislators believed that the information obtained from the survey made by Jones and Brown in 1857 was sufficient.[7]

After appointing members to the joint commission of 1860, the United States made no effort to maintain its claim to the disputed area, nor did it attempt to counteract the actions of Texas. In 1884 soldiers from Fort Sill in the Indian Territory were dispatched to eject any settlers from the disputed area. Finding several families and more than fifty thousand head of cattle from Texas in the area, the commander of the force, Lieutenant C. J. Crane, announced that the settlers must leave or be ejected.[8]

A month after Crane's warning, on July 1, 1884, President Chester Arthur issued a similar statement. The problem that had been ignored by the United States for almost twenty-five years suddenly was important. To settle the dispute, Congress created another joint commission in January, 1885.[9]

The commission met in Galveston, Texas, in February, 1886. The delegation from Texas was led by John T. Brackenridge, while the United States party was chaired by Major Samuel N. Mansfield. Other members from Texas were William S. Herndon, G. R. Freeman, and William H. Burgess. Members from the United States were A. R. Livermore, Thomas Casey, and Lansing Beach. All the commissioners appointed by the United States were members of the army, whereas the members from Texas were a mixture of politicians, businessmen, and government officials.[10]

The primary goals of the commission were to determine where the 100th meridian crossed the Red River and which fork of the Red River was the main branch referred to on the Melish map. To attain these goals, the commissioners collected twenty-three maps and various explorers' reports and called several witnesses, including Marcy, who had created the controversy by discovering the two forks of the Red in 1852.[11]

Marcy, now seventy-four years old and a retired general, was the first witness to testify. He appeared on February 26. Begging the commissioners' forgiveness for his lapses of memory, he referred them to his report of the exploration for the relationship between his knowledge of the area and the Melish map. He noted that "I have this morning for the first time, seen a copy."[12] After studying the map he made extensive comments:

> Upon this map only one large fork of the Red fork of Red River is delineated, with one more northerly small affluent, which is not named, but may have been intended for the Washita River or Cache Creek. But none of the important southern tributaries, such as the Big Wichita [sic], Pease River, and the Prairie Dog Town River are delineated thereon, unless the stream marked as the "Rio San Saba," is designated for the Prairie Dog Town branch, and as the real Rio San Saba of Texas is 500 miles or thereabouts distant from this locality, it does seem improbable that if the maker of the map had any vague conception of the existence of such a stream as the Prairie Dog Town River, he might have intended this as such. It certainly runs as far as the section of the map shows it nearly in the direction of that branch of the Red River, and is put down as rising near the eastern border of the Staked Plain, but the small section of the map does not show where it runs.[13]

After establishing the various faults of the map, Marcy stated his opinion concerning the main branch of the river:

I regarded the Prairie Dog Town branch as the main Red River, for the reason that its bed was much wider than that of the North Fork. Although the water only covered a small portion of its bed, and as the sandy earth absorbed a good deal of the water it debouched from the canon through which it flows, it may not contribute any more water to the lower river than the North Fork. The Prairie Dog Town branch and the North Fork of Red River from their confluence to their sources are of about equal length, the former being 180 miles and the latter 177 miles in length.[14]

Despite his statement that he had "regarded the Prairie Dog Town branch as the main Red River," Marcy continued that on seeing the Melish map he had concluded that the North Fork "was what is designated upon Melish's map as 'Rio Roxo.' I doubt if the Prairie Dog Town River was ever known to civilized men prior to my exploration in 1852, and if it was ever mapped before then I am not aware of it."[15]

After his somewhat confused beginning, Marcy listed his reasons for assuming that the North Fork was the branch referred to in the Melish map. He noted that the country along the South or Prairie Dog Town Fork was harsh and forbidding. Remembering his days of thirst and hardship there, he noted that the waters of the South Fork were "so bitter and unpalatable that many of my men became sick from drinking it."[16] Thus he was not surprised "that little if anything should have been known of this repulsive region" before his exploration. Furthermore, the name of the river itself indicated to Marcy that the South Fork had not been explored or mapped before his journey. He stated:

It is very certain that the Prairie Dog Town River, was never delineated upon any of our maps or designated by any Spanish, French, or English name, as were most of the other streams in that country, and it was only known to the Indians, and possibly to some Mexican traders, as the "Keche-ah-qui-ho-no," a Comanche appelation, the significance of which the Delawares informed me.[17]

Marcy also commented that Mexican traders probably did not travel across the area "with their carts in their trading expedi-

163

tions from Santa Fe to Nacogdoches, especially when there was so good a route a little further north possessing all the requisites for prairie traveling."[18] Marcy gave his final reasons for considering the North Fork the branch indicated on the Melish map:

> The Rio Rojo or Roxo upon Melish's map is almost entirely south and west of the Witchetaw [sic] Mountains but in close proximity to them, which is in accord with my determination of the position of the North Fork, while there are no mountains upon the Prairie Dog Town Branch.
>
> The head of the Rio Roxo upon Melish's map is put down as in about latitude 37 while upon my map the true latitude is 25½; while the Prairie Dog Town River rises in about latitude 34½°; so that if his Rio Roxo was intended to represent the "Prairie Dog Town River," it would be 2½° of latitude too far north.[19]

After hearing Marcy's comments, the commission adjourned until March 3.[20] At the next meeting of the commission (which was delayed until March 4 by illness in the family of one of the members from Texas) the United States delegation issued a statement declaring that the South Fork of the Red was the main fork and should be designated as the branch referred to on the Melish map, noting that the surveys made in 1857 and 1860 had accepted that conclusion. The Texans denied the supposition and on March 11 suggested that the tools needed to determine the meaning of the Melish map were not available to the commissioners.[21]

After this exchange the commission meetings were spent reviewing historical documents, such as correspondence between John Quincy Adams and Luis de Onís, the reports of Zebulon Pike and Stephen H. Long, and the writings of George Bancroft and Alexander von Humboldt. Several more witnesses, including Hamilton P. Bee and John S. ("Rip") Ford, were heard. Finally the commissioners agreed to disagree. The federal delegation issued a statement on July 14, 1886, that concluded:

It is maintained by the Commission on the part of Texas that the North Fork is the main Red River of the treaty, because this stream was at that time well known to the farmers thereof, while the Prairie Dog Town Fork was wholly unknown. We [the commissioners from the United States], on the contrary, have shown that nothing was known of either of these streams at the time alluded to, and that for this reason the physical features of the question must be our only criterion in a true interpretation of the treaty.

Hence . . . we are of the opinion that this [the South Fork] should be considered as the true Red River of the treaty.[22]

The commissioners from Texas responded that the evidence offered in support of the North Fork had not been refuted but that those representing the United States persisted in designating the South Fork as the boundary and that therefore a conclusion could not be reached. On July 16, 1886, the commission adjourned, noting that the problem would have to be passed to some other tribunal.[23]

The commission had met for five months, heard many witnesses, and reviewed hundreds of documents, but it could not reach a decision. At the root of the problem were the interests of each party. Texas wanted Greer County, and the United States wanted Greer County. Neither group was willing to yield the disputed area, dismissing or disregarding sworn testimony and historical fact. Another means of settling the case was necessary—a judgment by the United States Supreme Court.

In May, 1890, by an act of Congress the newly opened Territory of Oklahoma was organized. Included in the bill were provisions for the judicial settlement of the Greer County dispute. On October 27, 1890, Attorney General W. H. Miller filed suit in the Supreme Court against the state of Texas, asking that Greer County be judged part of the United States and that the Prairie Dog Town Fork of the Red River be named the main branch of the river.[24]

The attorneys for the state of Texas, Augustus Garland,

165

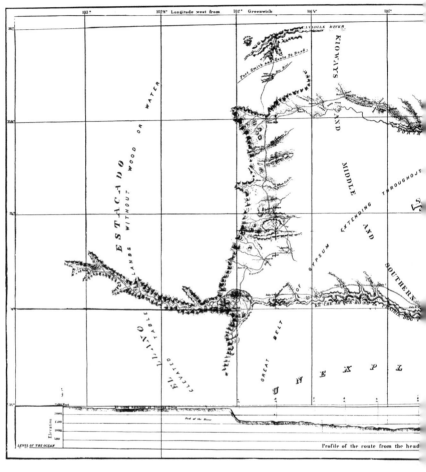

A map of the upper Red River in 1852, representing the region as Marcy and McClellan found it. From Captain Randolph B. Marcy and Captain

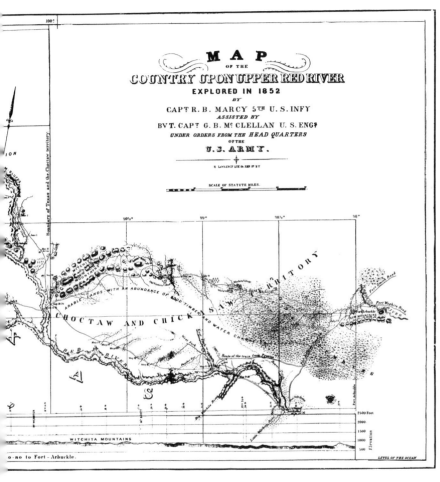

G. B. McClellan, *Adventure on Red River: A Report on the Explorations of the Headwaters of the Red River*, edited by Grant Foreman.

Charles A. Culberson, John Hancock, George Clark, and H. J. May, responded that the Supreme Court had no authority to accept the case because it was political in nature. They argued that the case involved settlement of a boundary dispute that had arisen from the treaty of 1819 and that such matters were the province of the executive and legislative branches; constitutionally the courts had no control over foreign relations of the United States or its boundary disputes. Furthermore, they said, the Supreme Court did not have jurisdiction in cases between the United States and individual states, noting that the Constitution did not specifically grant this power to the court.[25]

The court disagreed with all the Texans' assertions, noting that it inherently had jurisdiction over problems involving individual states. The fact that the matter had arisen from an international agreement did not alter the nature of jurisdiction. The Court ruled, in accepting the case brought by the United States, that if it did not have jurisdiction there were only three alternatives: mutual agreement, which had already failed; war, which was unacceptable to either side; or trial in a state court, which would abridge the sovereignty of the United States by placing it at the mercy of a state court.[26]

United States of America v. The State of Texas began on October 23, 1895, and ended on March 16 the following year. The court heard arguments, testimony, and statements and studied documents, maps, and reports, reviewing the same information that had been presented to the Boundary Commission of 1886. Representing the United States were Attorney General Judson Harmon, Solicitor General Holmes Conrad, and Edgar Allen, counsel for the plaintiff. Counsels for Texas were George Clark, M. M. Crane, A. H. Garland, Jr., J. H. May, Charles A. Culberson, and George Freeman.[27]

Beginning on October 23 and concluding on October 25, attorneys for both parties argued the merits of recognizing each fork of the river. In giving the decision of the court on

168

February 29, 1896, Associate Justice John M. Harlan reviewed
the historical background of the dispute, concluding:

. . . it is ordered, adjudged, and decreed that the territory east of
the 100th meridian of longitude, west and south of the river now
known as the north fork of Red river, and north of a line following
westward, as prescribed by the treaty of 1819 between the United
States and Spain, the course, and along the south bank, both of Red
River and of the river now known as the Prairie Dog Town fork or
south fork of Red River until such line meets the 100th meridian of
longitude,—which territory is sometimes called Greer County,—
constitutes no part of the territory properly included within or rightfully belonging to Texas at the time of the admission of that state
into the Union, and is not within the limits nor under the jurisdiction of that state, but is subject to the exclusive jurisdiction of the
United States of America. [28]

It appeared to the court that the intent of the treaty of 1819
was most clearly fulfilled by designating the South Fork as the
main branch of the Red River. All subsequent actions, such as
the organization of the county by Texas, the placing of the
county under the jurisdiction of the courts of Texas, and
claims to ownership of lands in the county by individuals, did
not alter the facts of the original case. Thus the court found
for the plaintiff, the United States. Texas, having for many
years believed that it was the rightful owner of the area, was
deprived of the region north of the South Fork and east of the
100th meridian. Undoubtedly, had Luís de Onís been alive in
1896, he would have been both pleased and amused by the
confusion and difficulty the treaty he so unwillingly had made
had caused the pushy, disrespectful Americans. [29]

All that remained to be settled in the long-standing dispute
was the designation of the point where the 100th meridian
crossed the Prairie Dog Town Fork—now the main fork—of
the Red River. On January 15, 1901, Congress directed Secretary of the Interior E. A. Hitchcock to cause "to be established and fixed the intersection of the true meridian with Red

169

River, or what . . . was known as the South Fork of Red River."[30] To fulfill this directive, Secretary Hitchcock dispatched Arthur D. Kidder, examiner of surveys, to find the point in question.[31]

Several attempts had been made to find the 100th meridian, including those of Jones and Brown in 1857, John H. Clark in 1858, C. L. Du Bois in 1873, O. T. Morrill also in 1873, H. C. F. Hackbusch in 1875, and Ehud N. Darling also in 1875. The accuracy of all these determinations was in question. Thus in 1903, after studying the findings of the previous surveys, Kidder set out to determine the exact point of intersection. He was also to determine the Texas–New Mexico and Texas–Oklahoma boundaries from the Red River to the Río Grande. In 1904 he reported that his work was concluded, noting that the previous survey of the 100th meridian's intersection with the Red had been less accurate than his because of recent improvements in astronomical instruments. He also noted that the Red River's periodic meandering made exact surveys of its course difficult. Thus the Greer County dispute ended, not with gunfire and sword but with a court decision and a surveyor's report.[32]

The end of the Greer County affair did not terminate the controversy over the Red River. While the Supreme Court had ruled that the line ran along the South Fork, the exact location of the boundary of the two states along the Red River had never been determined. Surely the line followed the Red, but it was one thing to draw lines on paper and another to draw lines across the face of the earth, especially along a river that shifted as often as the Red did.[33]

There seemed no urgent need to clarify the boundary at that time. In 1918, however, the situation changed drastically. Oil was discovered in Oklahoma, and large deposits were found under the bed of the Red River. Both Oklahoma and Texas wanted some of it—or all of it. Immediately after the discovery the state of Oklahoma began leasing portions of the riverbed. The state asserted ownership to the entire bed of the

Red River because of the Supreme Court's judgment of 1896 that the boundary followed the south bank of the river. The Lone Star State had not overtly disputed this assertion until the discovery of oil, when it began contending that the boundary followed the middle of the river and that the south half of the riverbed, along with the soil under it, belonged to Texas. Complicating the issue was a claim by the Comanches that the northern half of the river rightfully was theirs because the treaty of 1867 had granted to their tribe the territory extending to the middle of the river. Some citizens claimed that the riverbed was open to placer mining because the area had become federal land after the opening of the Big Pasture Indian Reservation in 1906, asserting that the Indians had forfeited all rights to the riverbed by accepting the reservation. Landowners along the river claimed ownership of the riverbed adjacent to their property.[34]

The Texas legislature passed an act providing for a suit to be brought against Oklahoma. The case was to be heard in the Supreme Court or in any court that officials of the state determined suitable. Quickly the matter deteriorated into a farce. The courts of both states assumed jurisdiction, and national guard units were called out, not to keep the peace but to support the claims of their respective sides.[35]

In 1919, Oklahoma moved to clarify—and, it was hoped, end—the disagreement by filing suit in the Supreme Court, asking the court to state that the boundary followed the south bank of the river. The Court immediately appointed a receiver to maintain oil and gas wells already in operation until the dispute was settled. To protect the rights of Indian claimants as well as its own interests, the United States entered the case by permission of the Court.[36]

In December, 1920, *State of Oklahoma v. State of Texas, United States of America, Intervenor* opened before the Supreme Court. Arguments were heard on the fourteenth and fifteenth of that month. Representing the various claimants were S. P. Freeling, attorney general of the state of Okla-

171

homa; C. M. Cureton, attorney general of the state of Texas; J. Garnett, assistant attorney general of the United States; and Joseph W. Bailey and A. H. Carrigan, attorneys for landowners.[37]

Oklahoma's legal representative contended that the boundary had been determined by judgment in the case concerning Greer County in 1896, when the Court had ruled that the boundary followed the course of the Red River "along the south bank"[38] The attorneys for Texas argued that the judgment had not been final because it had applied only to Greer County and that the treaty of 1819 the basis for the ruling, had been misconstrued. This contention arose from the vague wording of the treaty. The third article of the treaty read in part:

> The Boundary line between the two Countries, West of the Mississippi, shall begin on the Gulph [sic] of Mexico, at the mouth of the River Sabine in the Sea, continuing North, along the Western Bank of that River, to the 32d degree of Latitude, where it strikes the Rio Roxo of Natchitoches, or Red-River, then following the course of the Rio-Roxo Westward to the degree of Longitude, 100 West from London and 23 from Washington, then crossing the said Red-River, and running thence by a Line due North to the River Arkansas, thence, following the Course of the Southern bank of the Arkansas to its source in Latitude, 42. North, and thence by that parallel of Latitude to the South Sea . . . all the islands in the Sabine and the said Red and Arkansas Rivers, throughout the course thus described, to belong to the United States.[39]

According to the treaty, the boundary did indeed follow the west bank of the Sabine and the south bank of the Arkansas, but no such designation was made regarding the Red. The statement that all islands in the Red belonged to the United States implied that the entire bed of the river had been ceded to the Americans. Nonetheless, Texas contended that the wording of the treaty left the matter open to dispute.[40]

The Court issued its opinion on April 11, 1921. It noted that the Court was faced with two questions: Was the ruling of

1896 valid for the entire course of the river between Oklahoma and Texas, and did the treaty of 1819 intend the line to
follow the south bank or the middle of the Red River? If the
answer to the first question was affirmative, the second question was moot. The findings of the Court, in part, were

that, in elucidation of the matter, the treaty, and much historical
evidence of the negotiations that led up to it, were introduced, discussed by counsel in argument, and referred to in the opinion of the
court in 1896: and that the point was directly determined by the
court and the determination made part of its final decree. By every
test that properly can be applied, the matter is res judicata [deter-
mined by legal precedent].[41]

Therefore the state of Texas had no claim to any part of the
riverbed.

The matter was not yet settled, however. The United
States contested Oklahoma's claim to the entire bed of the
river, claiming ownership of the south half for itself and par-
tial ownership of the north half for itself and for members of
the Comanche, Kiowa, and Apache tribes. The question of
determining the meaning of the word "bank" regarding the
Red River was unanswered. Was the bank the high-water
mark or the low-water mark? What of the meanderings of the
river? When the river formed a cutoff, moving the channel
north or south, did the boundary follow the river?[42]

The claims of placer mines were discounted on May 1,
1922. The Court held that the portion of the river had never
been subject to mining claims because of its ownership by the
Indian tribes under the treaty of 1867.[43]

The state of Oklahoma argued that its ownership of the
riverbed arose from two factors: riparian right of the state as
the owner of public lands along the river granted to the state
on its entrance into the Union, and retention of ownership of
the riverbed because the Red was a navigable stream. Counsel
for Oklahoma argued that several acts by the federal government, such as authorizing bridges to be built on the Red River,

appropriation of funds to improve the river, and surveys of the river, as well as the assumption by Adams and Onís in making the treaty of 1819 that the Red River was navigable, demonstrated a previous acceptance of the navigability of the stream. Documents relating the frequent navigation of the river during the nineteenth century were offered as evidence of the historical navigability of the Red.[44]

Oklahoma's evidence for the navigability of the river was impressive. The Court ruled that, while the government had attempted to improve navigability above Fulton, Arkansas, and that while for a time the traffic on the river had been heavy, the situation had changed by 1920. The Corps of Engineers had ceased work on the river, and commerce was negligible. Therefore the Red no longer was a navigable waterway. The United States owned the lower half of the riverbed. The Court did allow the claim of the state to ownership of certain parts of the north half of the riverbed because of riparian right. The Court recognized the rights of various individuals, however, to riparian ownership of lands obtained from former Indian grants.[45]

The only matter left before the Court was the settlement of the definition of "banks." The United States and the state of Oklahoma contended that the intention of the treaty makers was the high-water mark of the river. Texas, however, claimed that the bank was the low-water mark, contending that the high-water mark would give the United States and Oklahoma almost half a million acres of Texas soil, soil that had been cultivated and held by Texans without dispute until the discovery of oil.[46]

Referring to the treaty of 1819 once more, the Court ruled that the drafters had specifically noted the boundary as running on the "respective Banks" of the rivers involved; thus the boundary followed the most easily recognizable bank of the Red River. That was, in the opinion of the Court, the "cutbank" where the water had eroded the earth. That was the high-water mark. These banks confined the waters of the river except during floods. As for changes in the course of the river, the boundary followed the river. For instance, when the river divided its waters, forming an island, the boundary ran along the north edge of the island.[47]

Arthur D. Kidder and Arthur A. Stiles were appointed by the court to survey the "south bank" of the Red, marking the boundary as it was in 1921. The survey was to begin at the "Big Bend" of the river and progress westward, ending at the 100th meridian.[48]

A supplement to this ruling was allowed by the Court on March 12, 1923, providing for protection of the riparian right of landowners to the middle of the river unless specifically limited by the court. Owners whose rights had been nonriparian when Kidder and Stiles made their survey and had since become riparian were granted ownership to the middle of the river. The receiver was ordered to surrender all patents and allotted tracts as quickly as possible.

In June, 1924, the Court ordered the receiver to audit his accounts and pay the necessary taxes on the profits earned. A year later, on June 1, 1925, all tracts were returned to their rightful owners.[49]

The only matter still undecided was the final marking of the boundary by Stiles and Kidder. Working from late 1923 until the summer of 1926, the men marked the designated boundary, and in April of 1927 the court approved the report.[50]

Thus, after approximately one hundred years, the dispute over ownership of the Red River finally ended. For more than two centuries nations and states had argued over the boundary of the Red, first France and Spain, then Spain and the United States, later the United States and Texas, and finally Texas and Oklahoma. The settlements had ranged from pragmatic agreements, such as those made by St. Denis and Aguayo in 1719 and Wilkinson and Herrera in 1806, to judicial decrees, such as those by the Supreme Court in 1896 and 1921. Two

175

hundred years had altered the method of settling disputes about the Red River, but not its nature. By the time the Court approved the final boundary decision, Congress was devising plans to tame the river.

11.

Taming the River

For countless centuries the Red River swelled with rainwater, rising each spring and falling each autumn. Occasionally this gentle pattern of nature was disrupted by particularly heavy or light rainfall, causing the river either to flood or to remain too low for commercial use. Sometimes there was just enough water, frequently there was too little, and sporadically there was too much. Man was the seemingly helpless victim of nature's moods. In the latter part of the 1930s, Congress relieved the plight of people in the Red River valley.

The River and Harbor Act of 1927 provided for a study of the advisability of improving the various rivers of the United States for purposes of navigation. In 1928 the Flood Control Act ordered studies of possible flood-control measures. Prospects for power-generation facilities were also to be studied.[1] The Red River was specifically mentioned in both bills.

Flood-control projects were needed in three major areas along the Red: the lowlands surrounding the mouth of the river, which were often flooded with backwaters from the Mississippi; the area near the mouth of the Ouachita River, which flooded with the Red and Ouachita crested; and low-lying regions along the river that flooded during high-water periods. In 1934, as a result of the two acts of Congress, the President's Committee on Water Flow suggested a series of dams and locks on the Red at fifty-two locations. These projects, the committee asserted, would effectively control flooding on the Red below Denison, Texas. The committee noted, however,

177

that the total cost of the projects would be prohibitive at that time. It was the opinion of the committee that only two projects should be considered immediately: dams at Columbia and Jonesville, Louisiana. The estimated cost of the dams was $395,000 and $443,000, respectively. Projects for the region near the mouth of the Red were to be delayed until work on the Mississippi River had been completed. As for projects on the upper Red, the committee found that the estimated cost made them "not appear to be justified at this time." Despite the committee's suggestion, Congress failed to approve any of the projects until the late 1930s.

In compliance with the acts the Army Corps of Engineers made a detailed report to Congress in January, 1936. The report dealt extensively with the physical makeup of the Red River and included recommendations concerning hydrology, navigation, flood control, irrigation, possibilities for power development, and estimated costs. The need for work on the Red River had long since been demonstrated by the destruction of thousands of dollars' worth of property in floods in 1908, 1927, and 1930. Moreover, commerce on the river had been restricted to the portion below Alexandria because of insufficient water upriver. With the passage of time the boats were too large for the shallow waters of the Red.[2]

After 1909, work on the Red by the Corps of Engineers had been limited to maintaining a six-foot channel below Alexandria. In the report of 1936 the corps advised Congress that the cost of extending the channel beyond Alexandria would be prohibitive, asserting that "the maximum value of a 6-foot project to Shreveport would not exceed $5,400,000. The lowest cost of such a project would be $40,000,000 or 26 times the value."[3] In light of this information the corps concluded that further work at that time was unadvisable, especially because there was little demand for waterborne transportation along the Red.[4]

The flood-control suggestions of the Corps of Engineers

were similar: although floods were a constant problem, the cost of providing adequate flood-control facilities for the area on the Red River were far more than the savings that could be realized. For example, in the corps's estimation "no project is justified unless the cost per acre providing flood protection is somewhat less than approximately $25."[5] In the area of the Rapides Islandes near Alexandria the cost per acre was $40.10. No area along the Red River was suitably situated or contained property sufficiently valuable to indicate the construction of flood-control facilities. Flood control on the Red River was delegated to the states.[6]

Recommendations concerning water power and irrigation projects were similarly negative. The corps noted that "the development of hydroelectric power in the basic would cost more than development of equivalent power from steam plants."[7] Again the cost-profit ratio was prohibitive. The average cost of constructing waterpower facilities on the Red were 8.10 mills per kilowatt-hour. In that time of plentiful and relatively inexpensive fuels for steam plants, the corps concluded that the development of hydroelectric power was nonessential. As for irrigation, the corps noted that "the present value of agricultural land does not justify such irrigation developments as are physically feasible."[8]

As a result of these reports, it was decided not to approve any new work on the Red River by the Corps of Engineers in 1936. Two years later, however, because of increased public pressure and increased demand for power, the Flood Control Act of 1938 authorized the corps to construct a dam on the Red near Denison, Texas, to aid in controlling floods on the Red and Washita rivers. Work began on the project early in 1939 and was completed in 1944. The dam, 15,200 feet long and 165 feet high, was five miles above Denison, just below the mouth of the Washita River. A year after the dam was finished, creating Lake Texoma, the first hydroelectric turbine was fitted into the structure, and four years later another generator was installed, bringing the total output of the unit to seventy thousand kilowatts per hour. The total cost of the project was almost $80 million.[9]

In the meantime Congress had acted again. From 1938 to 1944 several bills were passed requesting the Corps of Engineers to reevaluate the potential for further flood control and hydroelectric facilities on the Red River. The corps was directed to study the feasibility of opening a waterway from Jefferson, Texas, to Shreveport, Louisiana, as well as improving the navigability of the Red to Denison, Texas.[10] In 1946 the corps responded with two reports, one concerning navigability and the other regarding flood control and hydroelectric facilities. The latter recommended the construction of a series of dams on the Red and several of its tributaries, at a cost of more than $70 million. The former proposed radical modifications in existing plans for improving the navigability of the Red River:

. . . modification of the existing project . . . to provide for a channel 9 feet deep and 100 feet wide, extending from the Mississippi through . . . Red River, thence by a lateral canal leaving Red River through its right bank, at or near mile 31, and extending through land cuts and existing waterways, across the Mississippi-Red River backwater area and along the south bank of the Red River flood plain to Shreveport, by the construction of locks and dams and channel excavation.[11]

The total cost of this project was estimated at $42 million for construction and $600,000 a year for maintenance.[12]

Congress reacted favorably to the proposal for construction of flood-control and hydroelectric dams on the Red, delaying action on the proposed waterway to Shreveport on the grounds that the amount of commerce in the area along the Red did not warrant the expenditure of $40 million, at least not at that time. Congress, however, appropriated $77 million for construction of the dams proposed in the Flood Control Act of 1946. More than $100 million was appropriated for flood control and river improvement below Shreveport by the Mississippi River Commission. This appropriation resulted in the continued construction of jetties, dams, and levies on the lower river to prevent soil erosion and destruction of property by backwaters from the Mississippi.[13]

The Flood Control Act of 1946 was the beginning of serious efforts by the federal government to chain the forces of nature in the Red River valley, to prevent the destruction of property by the whims of the river, and to harness its seemingly limitless power. Yet it was only a first step. In 1950, Congress approved a flood-control act similar to the previous bill but larger in scope, asking for individual studies of the rivers of the nation and providing for individual appropriations.[14] It called for studies and projects in such areas as hydroelectricity, irrigation, navigation, water-quality, and flood-control improvements. Thereafter the work of the Corps of Engineers on the Red River was constant and extensive. More than 150 large projects had been proposed, were in progress, or had been completed by 1957.

Above Denison Dam the projects were designed mainly for three purposes: irrigation, municipal water supply, and hydroelectric production. Dams were constructed on the Washita, Pease, and Wichita rivers. Smaller dams and other water-flow-retardation devices, such as spillways and jetties, were constructed in areas of excessive soil erosion. By 1957 almost five hundred such smaller projects had been proposed or were in progress.[15]

Below Denison Dam most of the corps's work was directed toward flood control and water storage, with irrigation and prevention of soil erosion as adjuncts to the larger projects. In the early 1950s the corps revived the proposed canal system on the Red River below Shreveport to reopen navigation on the river to that city. The project was approved by Congress in 1965, but actual construction was delayed indefinitely. In 1967 the corps proposed an enlargement of the project, extending the canal-and-lock system to Jefferson, Lone Star, and Texarkana, Texas. Proposed as a long-range project that would not be instituted until conditions such as population size, industrial growth, and commercial activity in the affected areas warranted extensive outlays of money, the plan was designed to utilize related projects to hold costs to a minimum. The extension of the canal would be made by way of Twelve Mile, Black, and Kelly bayous; Caddo Lake; and Cypress Creek to reach Jefferson and Lone Star, the latter an industrial center in east Texas. The connection to Texarkana would be made by way of the Sulphur construct. The problem of maintaining a constant water level in the canal system was to be solved by utilizing proposed reservoirs as water-storage facilities. For the channel to Jefferson and Lone Star, a project was proposed called Ferrell's Bridge Reservoir (later known as the Lake O'Pines), to be used "for storing water to maintain pool levels." Texoma and Texarkana lakes would be used to regulate water flow for the channel to Texarkana.[16]

During the 1950s and 1960s, Congress continually approved appropriations for the construction of dams and reservoirs on the Red River and its tributaries. Additions to the Flood Control Act were made both specifically—when the act was modified in July, 1955, to include the Ferrell's Bridge Reservoir project—and generally—as with the passage of the rivers-and-harbors acts of 1958 and 1962.[17] The 1958 act provided that "the general plan for flood control on Red River, . . . as authorized by the Flood Control Act of 1946, is now modified and expanded, at an estimated cost in addition to that now authorized of $53,235,000."[18] This appropriation, added to minor appropriations between 1946 and 1958, raised the total amount of funds authorized by Congress for improvements on the Red River to almost $150 million. Four years later, in October, 1962, Congress approved an additional appropriation of $76,058,000 to be used to improve flood-control capabilities on ten tributaries of the Red River in Texas, Louisiana, Arkansas, and Oklahoma. Included in the 1962 act was an appropriation of $300,000 to construct two experimental water-quality studies in the Red River basin.[19] By 1970 several of the corps's major projects, such as the Broken Bow and Ferrell's Bridge reservoirs, had been completed; others, such as the Hugh and Boswell reservoirs, were under construction; still others, such as the proposed navigation channel to Shreveport, remained on the drawing board.[20]

One of the most successful corps projects was Lake Texoma, created by Denison Dam. The reservoir was designed to hold 5,382,000 acre-feet of water, including more than 2 million acre-feet of storage space for floodwaters. In 1970 the Corps of Engineers estimated that the total savings gained from flood prevention since the dams had been completed in 1944 was $28,979,000. In addition, the two turbines at these facilities had produced 162,000 kilowatt-hours of electricity during fiscal year 1970, supplying power to most of the surrounding towns. Today the reservoir also supplies water to Denison, the Texas Power and Light Company, Texaco, the Red River Authority of Texas, and Atlantic Richfield Company.[21]

The Denison Dam–Lake Texoma project was also an example of another function of the corps' work on the Red River—that of providing recreation facilities. In 1955 more than 5 million people visited the area, and in 1970 the lake attracted 9,700,000 visitors as well as more than 10,000 pleasure boats.[22] Hundreds of thousands of waterfowl have used the waters of Lake Texoma.

From 1930 to 1970 millions of dollars were spent for improvement of the Red River and its tributaries. The result was a sharp decrease in the loss of property to floods and plentiful water supplies, adequate supplies of electricity, and countless hours of recreation. The Red River valley would never again be the same.

12.

Today and Yesterday

Today small children frolic beside the Red River, sailing toy boats and searching for lunkers. Looking over its waters, they see powerful boats of plastic and steel skimming the surface. The river is for recreation—a plaything to be enjoyed. But if they listen to the sounds of the river, they may still hear the echo of some long-dead Frenchman singing of far-off places, or along the banks they may find a long-forgotten rut made where an Indian canoe came ashore. If the river could speak, what a wonderous tale it would tell—a tale of wars and friendships, of floods and droughts, of brave men and cowards, of life and death. When man first crept out from the darkness of caves, daring to see the light, the Red River was old—"as old as the wind," said the Caddos.

The Red River, at some places beautiful and sparkling, fascinating to body and mind, and at other places turbid and ugly, uninviting to the eye or palate, was a highway of commerce for more centuries than man can remember. Men—red and white, great and small, good and evil—have plied the waters of this river, carrying goods to be traded. When waves of Europeans swept across the continent, many pioneers traveled the Red River.

Settlement and civilization have brought the taming of the Red. Now there are cities where once the lodges of Indians stood. Where St. Denis found a small gathering of Caddos in 1714, now stands Natchitoches, Louisiana, a town of more than twenty thousand people. On land once open and teeming with wildlife, now stands Shreveport, Louisiana, a modern and bustling city. Where once the buffalo searched for grass, now stands Wichita Falls, Texas. Where once the Red River merged with the Washita to flow unfettered to the Mississippi, now lies Lake Texoma.

The Red River today bears little resemblancae to the wild and quarrelsome stream that delayed Luís de Moscoso's journey to Mexico more than four centuries ago. Dozens of bridges span its waters, great turbines harness its power, and computers gauge its flow. Dams and jetties deter and restrict its wanderings; no longer can it change its channel. Huge reservoirs hold its waters, keeping it from its rendezvous with the Mississippi. But in the fullness of time the river continues, pulled ever downward by the determined, relentless power of gravity. After uncountable millennia, after thousands of man-made changes, the river still flows. It is a successful river—still fulfilling its function of carrying water to the sea.

Despite the changes that have taken place on and along the Red River, despite the passage of time and the death of generations, the river remains constant. Men still use its waters to ease the burdens of life. Whether used to transport furs or to light the streets of a city, the waters of the river endure, permanent in a changing world.

Notes

CHAPTER 1

1. Randolph B. Marcy, *Exploration of the Red River of Louisiana in the Year 1852*, U.S., Congress, Senate, Document no. 54, 32d Cong., 2d sess., pp. 45–46; George Bonnell, *Topographical Description of Texas*, pp. 17–19; *Development of Water and Land Resources of the Arkansas-White and Red River Basins*, U.S., Congress, Senate, Document no. 13, 85th Cong., 1st sess., pp. 61–62.

2. Marcy, *Exploration*, pp. 54–56; Walter P. Webb, ed., *The Handbook of Texas*, vol. 2, p. 328.

3. Martin S. Garretson, *The American Bison*; Marcy, *Exploration*, pp. 15, 27–28, 46–47.

4. Garretson, *The American Bison*, pp. 25ff.

5. *Red River, La., Ark., Okla., and Texas*, U.S., Congress, House, Document no. 378, 74th Cong., 2d sess., pp. 349–68.

6. Ibid., p. 27; Marcy, *Exploration*, pp. 16–20.

7. Marcy, *Exploration*, p. 15.

8. Ibid.

9. Ibid., pp. 8–9; Bonnell, *Texas*, pp. 18–19; Emma Estill-Harbour, "A Brief History of the Red River Country Since 1803," *Chronicles of Oklahoma*, vol. 16, no. 1 (March, 1938), pp. 58–85.

10. Webb, *Handbook of Texas*, pp. 753–54; Robert T. Hill, "The Topography and Geology of the Cross Timbers and Surrounding Regions in Northern Texas," *American Journal of Science*, 3d ser., vol. 33 (1887), pp. 34–49.

11. Muriel Wright, "Early Navigation and Commerce Along the Arkansas and Red Rivers in Oklahoma," *Chronicles of Oklahoma*, vol. 8, no. 1 (March, 1927), pp. 65–88.

12. *Red River, La., Ark., Okla., and Texas*, p. 29; *Arkansas-White and Red River Basins*, pp. 882–38.

13. *Arkansas-White and Red River Basins*, pp. 916–87; *Red River, La., Ark., Okla., and Texas*, pp. 20–21.

14. *Red River, La., Ark., Okla., and Texas*, pp. 20–21, 33–34.

15. W. C. Nunn, "The Caddoes," *Indian Tribes of Texas*, pp. 19–20; Frederick W. Hodge, ed., *Handbook of American Indians North of Mexico*, vol. 1, p. 179.

16. Nunn, "The Caddoes," *Indian Tribes of Texas*, pp. 19–34; Hodge, *Handbook of American Indians*, vol. 1, p. 179.

187

17. Hodge, *Handbook of American Indians*, vol. 1, pp. 179–83.
18. Billy M. Jones, "The Wichitas," *Indian Tribes of Texas*, pp. 169–78; Hodge, *Handbook of American Indians*, vol. 2, pp. 947–50.
19. Hodge, *Handbook of American Indians*, vol. 2, pp. 947–48.
20. Ibid., pp. 768–69; Sandra L. Myres, "The Lipan Apache," *Indian Tribes of Texas*, pp. 122–45.
21. Hodge, *Handbook of American Indians*, vol. 1, p. 768.
22. Ernest Wallace and E. Adamson Hoebel, *The Comanches: Lords of the South Plains*; Hodge, *Handbook of American Indians*, vol. 1, pp. 327–29.
23. Hodge, *Handbook of American Indians*, vol. 1, p. 327; Wallace and Hoebel, *Comanches*, pp. 35–42.
24. See Rupert N. Richardson, "The Comanches," *Indian Tribes of Texas*, p. 41.

CHAPTER 2

1. See George P. Hammond and Agapito Rey, eds., *Narratives of the Coronado Expedition, 1540–1542*; Richard Hakluyt, trans., and William B. Rye, ed., *The Discovery and Conquest of Terra Florida by Don Ferdinando de Soto and Six Hundred Spaniards His Followers*, pp. 131–35.
2. Robert C. Clark, "The Beginnings of Texas," *Quarterly of the Texas State Historical Association*, vol. 5, no. 3 (January, 1902), pp. 171–75; Odie B. Faulk, *A Successful Failure*, pp. 39–59.
3. Melville B. Anderson, ed., *Joutel's Journal of La Salle's Last Voyage*, pp. 7ff.; for La Salle's life see Francis Parkman, *La Salle and the Discovery of the Great West*; see also Robert S. Weddle, *Wilderness Manhunt: The Spanish Search for La Salle*.
4. Anderson, *Joutel's Journal*, pp. 15–22.
5. Ibid.; William E. Dunn, *Spanish and French Rivalry in the Gulf Region of the United States, 1678–1702*, University of Texas Bulletin no. 1705, January 20, 1917, Studies in History no. 1, pp. 31–48.
6. Dunn, *Spanish and French Rivalry*, pp. 51–58.
7. Ibid., pp. 59–109; Weddle, *Wilderness Manhunt*, pp. 62ff.; Clark, "Beginnings of Texas," pp. 175–76; Elizabeth H. West, "De León's Expedition of 1689," *Quarterly of the Texas State Historical Association*, vol. 8, no. 3 (January, 1905), pp. 199–224.
8. West, "De León's Expedition," pp. 176–80; Dunn, *Spanish and French Rivalry*, pp. 111–29; Damián Manzanet, "Carta de don Damián Manzanet a don Carlos de Siquienza sobre el descubrimiento de la Bahía del Espíritu Santo," *Quarterly of the Texas State Historical Association*, vol. 2, no. 4 (April, 1899), pp. 254–80, English trans. Lilia A. Casis, pp. 281–312.
9. Manzanet, "Carta," pp. 254–80; Dunn, *Spanish and French Rivalry*, pp. 110–44; Bethel Coopwood, "Notes on the History of La Bahía and del Espíritu Santo," *Quarterly of the Texas State Historical Association*, vol. 2, no. 2 (October, 1898), pp. 162–69.
10. Dunn, *Spanish and French Rivalry*, pp. 140–44.
11. Ibid., pp. 185–215; Isaac J. Cox, "The Louisiana-Texas Frontier," *Quarterly of the Texas State Historical Association*, vol. 10, no. 1 (July, 1906), pp. 1–75; Charles B. Reed, *The First Great Canadian: The Story of Pierre le Moyne, Sieur d'Iberville*, pp. 186ff.

12. Clark, "The Beginnings of Texas," pp. 175–78; Pierre Margry, ed., *Découvertes et etablissements des français dans l'ouest et dans le sud de l'Amérique Septentrionale*, vol. 4, pp. 430–37.

13. Robert C. Clark, "Louis Juchereau de Saint-Denis and the Re-establishment of the Tejas Missions," *Quarterly of the Texas State Historical Association*, vol. 6, no. 1 (July, 1902), pp. 1026; Charmoin C. Shelby, "St. Denis's Declaration Concerning Texas in 1717," *Southwestern Historical Quarterly*, vol. 26, no. 3 (January, 1923), pp. 165–68; Lester G. Bugbee, "The Real Saint-Denis," *Quarterly of the Texas State Historical Association*, vol. 1, no. 4 (April, 1898), pp. 216–81; E. J. P. Schmitt, "Who was Juchereau de Saint-Denis?" ibid., vol. 1, no. 3 (January, 1898), pp. 204–15.

14. Edmund R. Murphy, *Henry de Tonty: Fur Trader of the Mississippi*, pp. 64ff.

15. Reed, *The First Canadian*, pp. 196–208.

16. Ibid.

17. Clark, "Saint-Denis," pp. 6–20; Margry, *Découvertes*,vol. 4, pp. 487–539, vol. 5, pp. 420–22, 498; Ross Phares, *Cavalier of the Wilderness*, pp. 23ff.

18. Clark, "Saint-Denis," pp. 14–15.

19. Ibid., pp. 15–17; Shelby, "St. Denis's Declaration," pp. 165–71; Milton Dunn, "History of Natchitoches," *Louisiana Historical Quarterly*, vol. 3, no. 1 (January, 1920), pp. 26–56; Phares, *Cavalier of the Wilderness*, pp. 52–58.

20. Clark, "Saint-Denis," pp. 20–25.

21. Ibid., pp. 25–31.

22. Shelby, "St. Denis's Declaration," pp. 168–74; Herbert E. Bolton, "Native Tribes About the East Texas Missions," *Quarterly of the Texas State Historical Association*, vol. 11, no. 4 (April, 1908), pp. 249–76.

23. Charmoin C. Shelby, "St. Denis's Second Expedition to the Rio Grande, 1716–1719," *Southwestern Historical Quarterly*, vol. 27, no. 3 (January, 1924), pp. 190–216; Margry, *Découvertes*, vol. 5, pp. 527–32; Bugbee, "Saint-Denis," p. 275.

CHAPTER 3

1. See Ross Phares, *Cavalier of the Wilderness*, pp. 143ff.; Pierre Margry, ed., *Découvertes et etablissements des français dans l'ouest et dans le sud de l'Amérique Septentrionale*, vol. 6, pp. 198–213; Isaac J. Cox, "The Louisiana-Texas Frontier," *Quarterly of the Texas State Historical Association*, vol. 10, no. 1 (July, 1906), pp. 9–30.

2. Charles Gayarre, *Louisiana: Its Colonial History and Romance*, pp. 197ff.; H. Montgomery Hyde, *John Law: The History of an Honest Adventurer*, pp. 57–68.

3. Hyde, *John Law*, pp. 79–100.

4. Gayarre, *Louisiana*, pp. 211–21.

5. Ibid.; Hyde, *John Law*, pp. 79ff.

6. Walter P. Webb, ed., *The Handbook of Texas*, vol. 2, p. 8.

7. See Cox, "Louisiana-Texas Frontier," p. 11; Margry, *Découvertes*, vol. 6, pp. 217ff.; Anna Lewis, *Along the Arkansas*, p. 33.

8. Lewis, *Along the Arkansas*, pp. 33–34; Margry, *Découvertes*, vol. 6, pp. 243–54.

9. Quoted in Lewis, *Along the Arkansas*, p. 34; Margry, *Découvertes*, vol. 6, pp. 255–67; La Harpe to Martin de Alarcón, in ibid., p. 267.

10. Margry, *Découvertes*, vol. 6, p. 266.

11. La Harpe to Pere Margil, ibid., p. 268; Cox, "Louisiana-Texas Frontier," p. 11.

12. Alarcón to La Harpe, May 20, 1719, quoted in U.S., Congress, *Annals of Congress*, 15th Cong., 2d sess., 1819, vol. 2, pp. 1777–78; La Harpe to Alarcón, July 8, 1719, ibid., p. 1778. La Harpe cheerfully wrote to Alarcón, "If you will do me the pleasure to come into this quarter, I will convince you I hold a post I know how to defend."

13. Margry, *Découvertes*, pp. 272–73.

14. Ibid., pp. 276–78.

15. Ibid., pp. 279–80.

16. Ibid.

17. Ibid., p. 280.

18. Ibid., pp. 280–99.

19. Odie B. Faulk, *A Successful Failure*, pp. 84–86.

20. Margry, *Découvertes*, pp. 300, 304–306; Blondel's letter quoted in ibid., p. 306.

21. Eleanor C. Buckley, "The Aguayo Expedition into Texas and Louisiana, 1719–1722," *Quarterly of the Texas State Historical Association*, vol. 15, no. 2 (October, 1911), pp. 1–65; Juan A. Morfi, *History of Texas, 1673–1779*, vol. 1, pp. 187–228.

22. Morfi, *History of Texas*, vol. 1, pp. 187–228.

23. Cox, "Louisiana-Texas Frontier," pp. 13–15.

24. Ibid., pp. 15–16.

25. See Lewis, *Along the Arkansas*, p. 61; Gayarre, *Louisiana*, pp. 220–32.

26. Cox, "Louisiana-Texas Frontier," pp. 15ff.

27. Ibid., pp. 16–18; Margry, *Découvertes*, vol. 4, pp. 543ff.; for River's report see Morfi, *History of Texas*, vol. 2, pp. 244–74.

28. Morfi, *History of Texas*, vol. 2, pp. 282–85.

29. Ibid., p. 285; Cox, "Louisiana-Texas Frontier," p. 20.

30. Cox, "Louisiana-Texas Frontier," pp. 20ff.; Morfi, *History of Texas*, pp. 285–95; Herbert Eugene Bolton, ed., *Athanase de Mézières and the Louisiana-Texas Frontier, 1768–1780*, vol. 1, pp. 17–61.

31. Margry, *Découvertes*, vol. 6, pp. 278–89.

32. Phares, *Cavalier of the Wilderness*.

33. Margry, *Découvertes*, vol. 6, pp. 280–99.

34. Ibid., pp. 357–82.

35. William E. Dunn, "Apache Relations in Texas," *Quarterly of the Texas State Historical Association*, vol. 14, no. 3 (January, 1911), pp. 198–274; Bolton, *De Mézières*, vol. 1, pp. 45–56.

36. Bolton, *De Mézières*, vol. 1, pp. 45–56; E. A. Harper, "The Taovayas in Frontier Trade and Diplomacy," *Chronicles of Oklahoma*, vol. 31, no. 3 (Autumn, 1953), p. 274.

37. Harper, "Taovayas," p. 274; Bolton, *De Mézières*, pp. 50–61.

38. Bolton, *De Mézières*, pp. 50–61.

39. Robert S. Weddle, *The San Sabá Mission: Spanish Pivot in Texas*, pp. 53–60; Morfi, *History of Texas*, pp. 371–72.

40. Morfi, *History of Texas*, vol. 2, pp. 61–71; Paul Nathan, ed. and trans., *The San Sabá Papers*, p. 104; William E. Dunn, "The Apache Mission on the San Sabá River," *Quarterly of the Texas State Historical Society*, vol. 17, no. 4 (April, 1914), pp. 379–414.

41. Weddle, *San Sabá*, pp. 72–78; Nathan, *San Sabá Papers*, pp. 95–97.
42. Nathan, *San Sabá Papers*, pp. 43–45, 73–77, 84–92; Weddle, *San Sabá*, pp. 72–84.
43. Weddle, *San Sabá*, pp. 118–28; Morfi, *History of Texas*, vol. 2, pp. 388–90.
44. Weddle, *San Sabá*, pp. 120–28; Morfi, *History of Texas*, vol. 2, pp. 390–91.
45. Bolton, *De Mézières*, pp. 66–68.

CHAPTER 4

1. See Herbert Eugene Bolton, ed., *Athanase de Mézières and the Louisiana-Texas Frontier, 1768–1780*, vol. 1, pp. 17–19, 66–79; Isaac J. Cox, "The Texas-Louisiana Frontier," *Quarterly of the Texas State Historical Association*, vol. 10, no. 2 (Summer, 1908) pp. 1–75.
2. Bolton, *De Mézières*, vol. 1, pp. 79–87. This work is a compilation of De Mézières's correspondence and reports. As such it provides a complete base for a study of his career.
3. Ibid.
4. Ibid.
5. De Mézières to Luis de Unzaga y Amezaga, February 1, 1770, ibid.; pp. 136–37; February 1, 1770, ibid.; pp. 140–142; May 20, 1720, ibid.; pp. 166–68; June 27, 1770, ibid.; pp. 202–203; Unzaga y Amezaga to De Mézières, September 20, 1770, ibid., p. 204.
6. De Mézières to Unzaga y Amezaga, September 27, 1770, ibid., pp. 204–205.
7. Ibid.
8. "Official Relation by the Lieutenant-Governor of Natchitoches to the Captain-General of Louisiana concerning the Expedition which, by Order of His Lordship, He Made to Cadodachos to Treat with the Hostile Tribes Whose Chiefs Met in that Village," report by De Mézières, October 29, 1770, ibid., p. 207.
9. Ibid.
10. Ibid., p. 209.
11. Ibid., pp. 210–11; "Deposition of Sergeant Domingo Chirinos," ibid., p. 223.
12. "Report, De Mézières," ibid., pp. 211–12.
13. Ibid., pp. 212–16.
14. Ibid., p. 220; "Deposition, Chirinos," ibid., pp. 223–24; "Deposition of Christobál Carabaxal," ibid., pp. 224–27; Unzaga y Amezaga to De Mézières, November 18, 1770, ibid., pp. 231–32; Joseph Gonzáles, "Exhortation sent to the Reverend Father President," ibid., pp. 227–28; Charles Raymond Cox, "Caddoan Relations with the White Race Previous to 1801" (master's thesis, Oklahoma State University, 1930), pp. 162–79; Herbert Eugene Bolton, *Texas in the Middle of the Eighteenth Century*, pp. 409–11.
15. "Official communication sent by the lieutenant-governor of Natchitoches, concerning the peace which the Apache are attempting to secure with other tribes, both of this district and that of Adaes, or Texas," De Mézières to Unzaga y Amezaga, February 25, 1772, Bolton, *De Mézières*, vol. 1, pp. 283–351.
16. Unzaga y Amezaga to De Mézières, April 23, 1773, ibid., vol. 2, pp. 31–32; ibid., vol. 1, p. 100.
17. Rogue de Medina to Hugo O'Conor, March 8, 1774, ibid., vol. 2, pp. 32–36;

Luís Antonio Menchaca to O'Conor, March 9, 1774, ibid., pp. 36–41; Rafael Martínez Pacheco to O'Conor, April 20, 1774, ibid., pp. 42–44; O'Conor to Antonio Bucareli y Ursua, April 20, 1774, ibid., pp. 44–46; O'Conor to Baron de Ripperda, April 21, 1774, ibid., pp. 46–49; De Ripperda to Unzaga y Amezaga, April 17, 1773, ibid., pp. 29–31.

18. J. Gaignard to Unzaga y Amezaga, January 6, 1774, ibid., pp. 81–82; J. Gaignard, "Journal Kept Exactly According to the Orders of M. de Villier to Make, with the Help of God and the Holy Virgin, the Journey at the Panis and Naytane, Begun at Natchitoche on the Day of My Departure October First, 1773," October 1, 1773, ibid., pp. 83–100.

19. J. Gaignard, "Journal," ibid., pp. 85–86.

20. Ibid.

21. Ibid.

22. Ibid.

23. Ibid., pp. 86–89.

24. Ibid., p. 87.

25. Ibid., pp. 88–100; Gaignard to Bernardo de Gálvez, November 10, 1777, ibid.; pp. 101–102.

26. Gaignard, "Journal," ibid., pp. 98–100; Unzaga y Amezaga to Baltazar Villeis, February 21, 1774, ibid., p. 102; De Mézières to Unzaga y Amezaga, June 30, 1774, ibid., pp. 104–108.

27. De Mézières to Croix, March 18, 1778, ibid., pp. 187–90.

28. Ibid.

29. De Mézières to Croix, April 18, 1778, ibid., p. 203.

30. Ibid., pp. 201–204.

31. Ibid.

32. Ibid.

33. De Mézières to Croix, April 19, 1778, ibid., pp. 204–207.

34. Ibid., p. 212.

35. Ibid., pp. 212–14.

36. Ibid.

37. De Mézières to Croix, May 2, 1778, ibid., pp. 214–16; Croix to De Mézières, September 10, 1778, ibid., pp. 216–18; Croix to Bernardo de Gálvez, September 10, 1778, ibid.; pp. 218–19; Croix to José de Gálvez, "The Commandant-General of the Interior Provinces of New Spain Reports the Successful Outcome of the Journey of Lieutenant-Colonel Don Atanasio DeMézières to the Northern Indian Nations," September 23, 1778, ibid., pp. 220–24; Croix, "Summary of the Notices Communicated to the Government in Sixteen Letters, by Don Atanasio de Mézières, Lieutenant-Governor of the Presidio of Natchitoches in the Colony of Louisiana, of the Results of the Expedition Which he Made to Visit the Northern Indian Nations," September 23, 1778, ibid., pp. 224–30.

38. De Mézières to Croix, May 2, 1778, ibid., pp. 215–16; Croix to De Mézières, September 10, 1778, ibid., pp. 216–17; De Mézières to Bernardo de Gálvez, February 7, 1779, ibid., pp. 239–40; March 17, 1779, ibid., p. 214; Bernardo de Gálvez to Croix, March 21, 1779, ibid., pp. 242–44; De Mézières to Croix, May 27, 1779, ibid., pp. 256–57; De Mézières to Bernardo de Gálvez, June 24, 1779, ibid., pp.

257–58; De Mézières to Croix, August 21, 1779, ibid., pp. 258–60; De Mézières to José de Gálvez, September 4, 1779, ibid., pp. 267–68; De Mézières to Croix, September 13, 1779, ibid., pp. 274–76; September 30, 1779, ibid., pp. 274–76; September 30, 1779, ibid., pp. 289–91; October 7, 1779, ibid., pp. 291–98; October 13, 1779, ibid., pp. 319–22; De Mézières to Matías de Gálvez, October 28, 1779, ibid., p. 324; De Mézières to Croix, n.d., ibid., pp. 324–25; Bachelor Pedro Fuentes y Fernández, "Record of the Burial of De Mézières," November 3, 1779, ibid., p. 327.

39. See Teodoro de Croix, "General Report of 1781," Croix to José de Gálvez, in Alfred Barnaby Thomas, trans. and ed., *Teodoro de Croix and the Northern Frontier of New Spain, 1776–1783,* pp. 74–83; Odie B. Faulk, "The Comanche Invasion of Texas, 1743–1836," *Great Plains Journal,* vol. 9, no. 1 (Fall, 1969), pp. 28–31.

40. Faulk, "Comanche Invasion," p. 29; Croix, "Report of 1781," Thomas, *Croix,* p. 80; "Estado de las tropas . . . provincias de Texas," Croix to Gálvez, June 27, 1783, ibid., p. 63.

41. Estado de las tropas . . . provincias de Texas, Thomas, *Croix,* p. 63.

42. Faulk, "Comanche Invasion," pp. 29–50.

43. Ibid., pp. 29–31; Noel M. Loomis and Abraham P. Nasatir, *Pedro Vial and the Roads to Santa Fe,* pp. 262–63; Carlos E. Castañeda, *Our Catholic Heritage in Texas,* vol. 5, pp. 158–61.

44. Loomis and Nasatir, *Pedro Vial,* pp. 262–65.

45. Ibid., pp. 265–66.

46. Ibid., pp. 262–65; see Castañeda, *Our Catholic Heritage,* vol. 5, pp. 148–51; see also Herbert Eugene Bolton, *Texas in the Middle Eighteenth Century,* p. 128.

47. Jacobo Urgarte y Loyola to J. B. de Anza, October 26, 1786 (New Mexico Archives).

48. "Diary of Pedro Vial, Bexar to Santa Fe, October 4, 1786, to May 26, 1787," in Loomis and Nasatir, *Pedro Vial,* p. 270–82.

49. Ibid., p. 281.

50. Ibid., p. 283–85.

51. Ibid., pp. 288–89; Castañeda, *Our Catholic Heritage,* vol. 5, pp. 146–47.

52. Castañeda, *Our Catholic Heritage,* vol. 5, pp. 146–47.

53. "Journal of José Mares, Santa Fe to Texas, July 31 to October 8, 1787," in Loomis and Nasatir, *Pedro Vial,* pp. 289–314.

54. Ibid., pp. 315–17.

55. "Diary of Santiago Fernández from Santa Fe to the Taovayas and Return to Santa Fe, June 24–July 21, 1788, and July 25–December 17, 1788," ibid., pp. 318–26; "Diary of Francisco Xavier Fragoso, Santa Fe to Natchitoches to San Antonio to Santa Fe, June 24, 1788–August 20, 1789," ibid., pp. 327–47.

56. "Diary, Fragoso," Loomis and Nasatir, *Pedro Vial,* pp. 327–39; "Diary, Fernández," ibid., pp. 318–19.

57. "Diary, Fernández," Loomis and Nasatir, *Pedro Vial,* pp. 319–26; "Diary, Fragoso," ibid., pp. 339–43.

58. "Diary, Fragoso," Loomis and Nasatir, *Pedro Vial,* pp. 345–61.

59. See Castañeda, *Our Catholic Heritage,* vol. 5, pp. 151–58, and map facing p. 267.

CHAPTER 5

1. Thomas Jefferson, *The Writings of Thomas Jefferson*, ed. Paul L. Ford, vol. 8, pp. 252–55; see also William Dunbar to Thomas Jefferson, n.d., William Dunbar, *Life, Letters, and Papers of William Dunbar*, ed. Eron Rowland, pp. 122–23; Dunbar to Jefferson, January, 1804, ibid., pp. 126–27; Henry Dearborn to Dunbar, April 4, 1804, ibid., p. 128; Dunbar to Jefferson, May 13, 1804, ibid., pp. 130–33; Dunbar to Jefferson, June 9, 1804, ibid., pp. 133–35; Isaac J. Cox, "The Exploration of the Louisiana Frontier, 1803–1806," *Annual Report of the American Historical Association for 1904*, pp. 151–66.

2. Dunbar to Peter Walker, June 10, 1804, Dunbar, *William Dunbar*, pp. 135–37; Dunbar to Constant Freeman, June 14, 1804, ibid., pp. 137–38; Cox, "Louisiana Frontier," pp. 159–61.

3. Cox, "Louisiana Frontier," pp. 159–61; Dearborn to Dunbar, May 24, 1805, Dunbar, *William Dunbar*, pp. 152–53; Dunbar to Jefferson, July 6, 1805, ibid., pp. 154–56; Jefferson to Dunbar, May 25, 1805, Jefferson, *Writings of Thomas Jefferson*, vol. 10, pp. 126–27; Andrew Wheat, *Mapping the American West: A Preliminary Study*, pp. 64–66.

4. See Marqués de Casa Calvo to Juan Bautista de Elquezabal, June 27, 1804 (Bexar Archives, University of Texas); Nemesio Salcedo y Salcedo to Casa Calvo, October 8, 1805 (Bexar Archives); Dunbar to Jefferson, July 6, 1805, Dunbar, *William Dunbar*, pp. 154–56; Salcedo to Antonio Cordero y Bustamente, October 8, 1805 (Bexar Archives).

5. Salcedo to Bustamente, October 8, 1805 (Bexar Archives).

6. Dearborn to John Sibley, December, 1804, Letterbook of the Natchitoches Indian Factory, Office of Indian Affairs; Thomas Jefferson, "Message from the President of the United States Communicating Discoveries Made in Exploring the Missouri, Red River and Washita by Captains Lewis and Clark, Doctor Sibley and Mr. Dunbar; with a Statistical Account of the Countries Adjacent, February 19, 1806," U.S., Congress, *Annals of Congress*, 9th Cong., 2d sess., 1805, pp. 1076–1105; Cox, "Louisiana Frontier," pp. 164–65.

7. Cox, "Louisiana Frontier," pp. 159–60.

8. Ibid., pp. 160–62.

9. Ibid.; Salcedo to Cordero, May 3, 1804 (Bexar Archives); Casa Calvo to Elquezabal, June 27, 1804 (Bexar Archives); for the attitude of the Spanish officials see Odie B. Faulk, *The Last Years of Spanish Texas*, pp. 119–27.

10. Elquezabal to Salcedo, August 29, 1804 (Bexar Archives); Salcedo to Cordero, January 1 and 28, 1806 (Bexar Archives); Cox, "Louisiana Frontier," pp. 167–68. Probably the exclusion of Casa Calvo had little effect on the attitude of Spanish officials. Salcedo had already demonstrated his dislike of foreigners, and Casa Calvo's passport would have made little difference. See Faulk, *Spanish Texas*, pp. 122–23.

11. Thomas Freeman and Peter Custis, *An Account of the Red River in Louisiana Drawn Up from the Returns of Messrs. Freeman and Custis to the War Office of the United States, Who Explored the Same in the Year 1806*. Unless otherwise noted, the remainder of the narrative regarding the expedition is taken from this work.

12. Salcedo to Sebastián Iturrigary, August 25, 1806 (Bexar Archives); Dionisio

Del Valle to Cordero, March 19, 1806 (Bexar Archives); Francisco Viana to Cordero, June 6, 1806 (Bexar Archives).

13. Cox, "Louisiana Frontier," p. 173.

14. See Faulk, *Spanish Texas*, p. 124; Miguel Serrano, "Estado que manifiesta la fuerze total y destinos de las tropas que existen en esta provincia," June 26, 1806 (Bexar Archives).

15. Serrano, "Estado" (Bexar Archives).

16. Walter Flavius McCaleb, *The Aaron Burr Conspiracy*, pp. 93ff.

17. James Wilkinson to Cordero, September 23, 1806 (Bexar Archives); Cordero to Wilkinson, September 29, 1806 (Bexar Archives).

18. McCaleb, *Burr Conspiracy*, pp. 111–17.

19. Ibid.

20. Wilkinson to Cordero, October 29, 1806 (Bexar Archives); Ernest Wallace and David M. Vigness, eds., *Documents of Texas History*, pp. 37–38; Simón de Herrera to Wilkinson, November 4, 1806, ibid., p. 38.

21. See "Relations with Spain," U.S., Congress, *Annals of Congress*, 9th Cong. 1st sess., 1805–1806, pp. 1156–1224; Philip C. Brooks, *Diplomacy and the Borderlands: The Adams-Onís Treaty of 1819*, pp. 1–28.

22. Brooks, *Diplomacy and the Borderlands*, p. 1–28.

23. George Dangerfield, *The Awakening of American Nationalism*; Brooks, *Diplomacy and the Borderlands*, p. 59.

24. See John Lynch, *The Spanish American Revolutions, 1808–1826*.

25. Brooks, *Diplomacy and the Borderlands*, pp. 13–14.

26. Ibid., pp. 15ff.

27. Ibid., pp. 71ff.; "Relations with Spain," U.S., Congress, *Annals of Congress*, 15th Cong., 2d sess., 1819, vol. 2, pp. 1658–70.

28. Brooks, *Diplomacy and the Borderlands*, pp. 57–70.

29. See Samuel Flagg Bemis, *John Quincy Adams and the Foundation of American Foreign Policy*.

30. Ibid.

31. See James Monroe to Luis de Onís, January 19, 1816, U.S., Congress, *Annals of Congress*, 15th Cong., 2d sess., 1819, vol. 2, pp. 1635–40; Onís to Monroe, February 22, 1816, ibid., pp. 1640–47; John Dick to Onís, June 10, 1816, ibid., pp. 1647–57; George Erving to Monroe, September 22, 1816, ibid., pp. 1661–67; Pedro Cevallos to Erving, n.d., ibid., p. 1667; Onís to Monroe, January 16, 1817, ibid., pp. 1668–70; Brooks, *Diplomacy and the Borderlands*, pp. 71ff.

32. Onís to John Quincy Adams, December 10, 1817, U.S., Congress, *Annals of Congress*, 15th Cong., 2d sess., 1819, vol. 2, pp. 1704–1705; Adams to Onís, December 16, 1817, ibid., p. 1705; Onís to Adams, December 29, 1817, ibid., pp. 1705–14; Onís to Adams, January 5, 1818, ibid., pp. 1714–27; Onís to Adams, January 8, 1818, ibid., pp. 1727–32.

33. Adams to Onís, January 16, 1818, ibid., pp. 1737–39; Onís to Adams, January 24, 1818, ibid., pp. 1739–46.

34. See Brooks, *Diplomacy and the Borderlands*, pp. 105–30.

35. Bemis, *John Quincy Adams*, pp. 179–83.

36. See Adams to Onís, March 12, 1818, U.S., Congress, *Annals of Congress*, 15th

Cong., 2d sess., 1819, vol. 2, pp. 1748–77; Onís to Adams, March 23, 1818, ibid., pp. 1780–98.

37. Onís to Adams, March 27, 1818, U.S., Congress, *Annals of Congress*, 15th Cong., 2d sess., 1819, vol. 2, pp. 1798–1804; Onís to Adams, May 7, 1818, ibid., pp. 1814–15; Onís to Adams, June 17, 1818, ibid., pp. 1818–19; Onís to Adams, June 24, 1818, ibid., p. 1819; Onís to Adams, July 8, 1818, ibid., pp. 1819–22; Onís to Adams, July 21, 1818, ibid., pp. 1822–23.

38. Onís to Adams, June 24, 1818, ibid., p. 1819; Onís to Adams, July 21, 1818, ibid., pp. 1822–23; Adams to Onís, July 23, 1818, ibid., pp. 1823–27; Brooks, *Diplomacy and the Borderlands*, pp. 137–42.

39. Negotiations were terminated during the summer after Jackson's invasion. In October, Spanish officials agreed to resume the talks; see Erving to José Pizarro, August 31, 1818, U.S., Congress, *Annals of Congress*, 15th Cong., 2d sess., 1819, vol. 2, p. 1887; Onís to Adams, October 18, 1818, ibid., pp. 1889–90; Adams to Onís, October 23, 1818, ibid., p. 1890; Onís to Adams, October 24, 1818, ibid., pp. 1890–1900; "Translation of Propositions Received in Mr. Onís's Letter of October 24, 1818," ibid., pp. 1900–1902.

40. Adams to Onís, October 31, 1818, ibid., pp. 1902–1906.

41. Onís to Adams, November 16, 1818, ibid., pp. 1906–12.

42. See correspondence in ibid., pp. 1930–2101; see also Brooks, *Diplomacy and the Borderlands*, pp. 148ff.

43. Brooks, *Diplomacy and the Borderlands*, pp. 154–55; Onís to Adams, December 12, 1818, and January 11 and 16, 1819, U.S., Congress, *Annals of Congress*, 15th Cong., 2d sess., 1819, vol. 2, pp. 2101–10; Adams to Onís, January 29, 1819, ibid., pp. 2110–11; Onís to Adams, February 1, 1819, ibid., pp. 2111–13; "Treaty Project," Onís to Adams, February 6, 1819, ibid., pp. 2114–19.

44. "Counter Project of a Treaty," Adams to Onís, February 13, 1819, ibid., pp. 2119–24.

45. See Brooks, *Diplomacy and the Borderlands*, pp. 158–65.

46. Ibid., pp. 205–14; "Treaty of Amity, Settlement, and Limits, Between the United States of America and His Catholic Majesty," U.S., Congress, *Annals of Congress*, 15th Cong., 2d sess., vol. 2, 1819, pp. 2129–35.

47. "Resolution of the Senate Advising Ratification," February 24, 1819, U.S., Congress, *Annals of Congress*, 15th Cong., 2d sess., 1819, vol. 2, p. 2135; "Ratification by the President of the United States," ibid., pp. 2135–36; Brooks, *Diplomacy and the Borderlands*, pp. 191ff.

CHAPTER 6

1. *Census for 1820* (Fourth Census), bk. 1, p. 31.

2. Emma Estill-Harbour, "A Brief History of the Red River Country Since 1803," *Chronicles of Oklahoma*, vol. 16, no. 1 (March, 1938), pp. 58–65.

3. See Odie B. Faulk, *The Last Years of Spanish Texas*, pp. 121–25.

4. Ibid.

5. Mattie Austin Hatcher, *The Opening of Texas to Foreign Settlement*, pp. 131–32; Carlos E. Castañeda, *Our Catholic Heritage in Texas*, vol. 6, pp. 291–93; Walter P. Webb, ed., *The Handbook of Texas*, vol. 1, pp. 80–81.

6. Harbour, "Red River Country," pp. 71–75.
7. Ibid.
8. Ibid.; Charles Thomas to Jefferson Davis, January 11, 1854, U.S., Congress, House, Document no. 24, 33d Cong., 1st sess.; Thomas S. Jessup to C. M. Conrad, December 20, 1851, ibid.
9. *Report of the Chief Engineer of the Army for 1873*, pp. 644–46.
10. "Letter from Dr. Joseph Paxton, of Hemstead County, to the Hon. A. H. Sevier, Delegate to Congress from the Territory of Arkansas, in Relation to the Raft of Red River," August 1, 1828, U.S., Congress, House, Document no. 78, 20th Cong., 2d sess. Paxton's letter is eighteen pages long; the following citations indicate numbers within the document.
11. Ibid., p. 10.
12. Ibid.
13. Ibid.
14. Ibid.
15. Ibid., p. 11.
16. Ibid., p. 12.
17. Ibid., p. 13.
18. Ibid., p. 14.
19. Ibid., p. 16.
20. Henry M. Shreve to Charles Gratiot, September 29, 1832, U.S., Congress, House, Document no. 98, 23d Cong., 1st sess.
21. Ibid.; *Report of the Chief Engineer of the Army for 1874*, pp. 704–709. The report includes a brief history of the early attempts to remove the raft; see also *Report of the Chief Engineer of the Army for 1901*, p. 1011; Charles Gratiot to Henry M. Shreve, September 5, 1832, U.S. Congress, House, Document no. 98.
22. Henry M. Shreve to Charles Gratiot, September 29, 1832, ibid.
23. Ibid.
24. Charles Gratiot to Henry M. Shreve, February 8, 1833, ibid.; Henry M. Shreve to Charles Gratiot, April 12, 1833, ibid.
25. Henry M. Shreve to Charles Gratiot, April 12, 1833, ibid.
26. Henry M. Shreve to Charles Gratiot, May 8, 1833, ibid.
27. Henry M. Shreve, "Report of Work Done at the Great Raft on Red River, Louisiana," ibid.
28. Ibid.
29. Ibid.
30. Ibid.
31. *Report of the Chief Engineer of the Army for 1901*, p. 1011.
32. Henry M. Shreve to Joseph G. Totten, June 12, 1839, U.S., Congress, House, Document no. 1, 25th Cong., 1st sess.
33. Ibid.
34. Thomas Jessup to Joel Poinsett, December 8, 1839, ibid.
35. Stephen H. Long to J. J. Albert, June 1, 1841, U.S., Congress, Senate, Document no. 64, 27th Cong., 1st sess. Long's letter is twenty-two pages long; the following citations indicate page numbers within the document.
36. Ibid., p. 21.
37. Ibid., pp. 17–22.

38. Charles Fuller to J. E. Johnston, January 18, 1855, U.S., Congress, Senate, Executive Document no. 62, 33d Cong., 2d sess.

39. *Report of the Chief Engineer for the Army for 1873*, pp. 644–49.

40. Charles Linnard, "Report of Work Done at Red River Raft," U.S., Congress, Senate, Document no. 37, 28th Cong., 1st sess.

41. *Report of the Chief Engineer of the Army for 1901*, p. 1011; Charles A. Fuller to J. E. Johnston, "Report of Survey of Red River, in the Region of the Raft," U.S., Congress, Senate, Executive Document no. 62, 33d Cong., 2d sess.; Charles A. Fuller to James Kearney, February 17, 1855 (supplementary report), ibid.

42. Ibid.

43. *The Seventh Census of the United States: 1850*, p. 474; Webb, *Handbook of Texas*, vol. 1, p. 909.

CHAPTER 7

1. See Zebulon Montgomery Pike, *The Expedition of Zebulon Montgomery Pike to Headwaters of the Mississippi River, Through Louisiana Territory, and in New Spain, During the Years 1805–6–7*, ed. Elliott Coues; Edwin James, *Account of an Expedition from Pittsburg to the Rocky Mountains, Performed in the Years 1819 and '20 by Order of the Hon. J. C. Calhoun, Sec'y of War: Under the Command of Stephen H. Long*, vols. 14–16 and 22 in Reuben Gold Thwaites, ed., *Early Western Travels*; Randolph B. Marcy, *Adventure on Red River*, ed. Grant Foreman, pp. 3–4.

2. Randolph B. Marcy, *Expedition of the Red River of Louisiana in the Year 1852*, U.S., Congress, Senate, Executive Document no. 54, 32d Cong., 2d sess., pp. 2–3. This document is Marcy's report on his exploration. Unless otherwise noted, the following narrative is taken from this report, and page numbers indicate pages within the document.

3. Ibid., pp. 2–5; see Marcy, *Adventure on Red River*, pp. v–vii.

4. Marcy, *Expedition*, pp. 4–8.

5. Ibid., p. 10.

6. Ibid., p. 11.

7. Ibid., pp. 10–11.

8. Ibid., p. 12.

9. Ibid., p. 14.

10. Ibid., p. 15.

11. Ibid., pp. 17–18.

12. Ibid., p. 18.

13. Ibid.

14. Ibid.

15. Ibid.

16. Ibid.

17. Ibid.

18. Ibid., p. 19.

19. Ibid., pp. 20–21.

20. Ibid., pp. 25–26.

21. Ibid., p. 27.

22. Ibid.

23. Ibid., pp. 27–28.
24. Ibid., p. 28.
25. Ibid., pp. 32–33.
26. Ibid., pp. 38–39.
27. Ibid., p. 39.
28. Ibid., pp. 40–41.
29. Ibid., pp. 45–48.
30. Ibid.
31. Ibid., p. 48.
32. Ibid., pp. 49–50.
33. Ibid., p. 50.
34. Ibid., pp. 50–51.
35. Ibid.
36. Ibid.
37. Ibid.
38. Ibid.
39. Ibid., p. 56.
40. Ibid.
41. Ibid.
42. Ibid., p. 53.
43. Ibid., pp. 53–54.
44. Ibid., p. 54.
45. Ibid., p. 55.
46. Ibid.
47. Ibid., p. 58.
48. Ibid., pp. 59–82.
49. Ibid., p. 82.

CHAPTER 8

1. For the background of the campaign see Ludwell H. Johnson, *Red River Campaign: Politics and Cotton in the Civil War*, pp. 1–48; for the events in Texas and Louisiana before the attack up the Red River see Carl Newton Tyson, "Texas: Men for War; Cotton for Economy," *Journal of the West*, vol. 14, no. 1 (January, 1975), pp. 130–48; Buford Satcher, "Louisiana: Six Hundred Engagements," ibid., pp. 149–66.

2. Alwyn Barr, "Texas Coastal Defenses, 1861–65," *Southwestern Historical Quarterly*, vol. 65, no. 1 (July, 1961), pp. 1–31; Tyson, "Texas," pp. 138–39; Confederate Reports, *The War of the Rebellion: A Compilation of the Official Records of the Union and Confederate Armies*, ser. 1, vol. 26, pt. 2, pp. 309–12, hereafter cited as *Official Records*; Union Reports, U.S. Department of the Navy, *Official Records of the Union and Confederate Navies in the War of the Rebellion*, ser. 1, vol. 20, pp. 517–61, hereafter cited as *Official Records, Navy*.

3. Tyson, "Texas," pp. 138–39; Nathaniel Banks to H. H. Bell, November 3, 1863, Nathaniel Banks to Francis J. Herron, December 25, 1863, *Official Records*, ser. 1, vol. 36, pt. 1, pp. 785, 880–81; John Magruder to Edmund Kirby-Smith, December 24, 1863, ibid., vol. 25, pt. 2, pp. 524–30.

4. Henry W. Halleck to Nathaniel Banks, January 4, 1864, *Official Records*, vol. 34, pt. 2, pp. 15, 42, 145.

5. Ibid.; Henry W. Halleck to Nathaniel Banks, December 7, 1863, ibid., vol. 31, pt. 1, pp. 683, 807; Nathaniel Banks to William S. Halleck, December 23, 1863, ibid., vol. 26, pt. 1, pp. 871–73; Johnson, *Red River Campaign*, pp. 75–77.

6. Nathaniel Banks to Henry W. Halleck, January 25, 1864, *Official Records*, vol. 34, pt. 2, pp. 140–52; Henry W. Halleck to Nathaniel Banks, April 11, 1864, ibid., vol. 34, pt. 2, p. 293.

7. For Sherman's estimate of Banks see William T. Sherman, *Memoirs of Gen. W. T. Sherman*, vol. 1, pp. 425–26.

8. Frederick Steele to Nathaniel Banks, February 18, 1864, *Official Records*, vol. 34, pt. 2, pp. 249–321.

9. U. S. Grant to Frederick Steele, March 15, ibid., vol. 34, pt. 2, p. 616.

10. David Porter to Nathaniel Banks, February 27, 1863, *Official Records, Navy*, vol. 26, pp. 747–48.

11. Johnson, *Red River Campaign*, p. 76; Allen Johnson and Dumas Malone, eds., *Dictionary of American Biography*, 20 vols. (New York: Charles Scribner's Sons, 1956), vol. 1, pp. 577–80.

12. Johnson and Malone, *Dictionary of American Biography*, vol. 1, pp. 577–80.

13. Ibid.

14. For an expression of the general estimation of Banks see Henry S. Halleck to William T. Sherman, April 8, 1864, *Official Records*, vol. 32, pt. 3, pp. 285–90; Johnson, *Red River Campaign*, p. 85.

15. Jefferson Davis Bragg, *Louisiana in the Confederacy*, pp. 20–25; Satcher, "Louisiana," pp. 157–58.

16. Tyson, "Texas," pp. 138–39.

17. Ibid.; Richard Taylor to Edmund Kirby-Smith, March 13, 1864, *Official Records*, vol. 34, pt. 1, p. 489.

18. Richard Taylor to Edmund Kirby-Smith, March 13, 1864, *Official Records*, vol. 34, pt. 1, p. 489.

19. John Dimitry, "Louisiana," in Clement A. Evans, ed., *Confederate Military History* (Atlanta, Ga.: Confederate Publishing Co., 1899), vol. 10, pp. 127–30.

20. Ibid.; Richard Taylor, *Destruction and Reconstruction: Personal Experiences of the Late War*, pp. 154–55.

21. Taylor, *Destruction and Reconstruction*, p. 153; Johnson and Malone, *Dictionary of American Biography*, pp. 340–41.

22. A. J. Smith to Nathaniel Banks, March 14, 1864, *Official Records*, vol. 34, pt. 1, p. 305; J. G. Walker to Richard Taylor, March 20, 1864, ibid., vol. 34, pt. 1, p. 599.

23. Evans, *Confederate Military History*, vol. 10, pp. 129–30.

24. A. J. Smith to Nathaniel Banks, March 15, 1864, *Official Records*, vol. 34, pt. 1, pp. 305–47.

25. Ibid.

26. Richard Taylor to Edmund Kirby-Smith, March 16, 1864, *Official Records*, vol. 39, pt. 1, pp. 506–20, 559–64.

27. Ibid.

28. U. S. Grant to Nathaniel Banks, March 24, 1864, *Official Records*, vol. 39, pt. 2, pp. 610–15. For the problems concerning routes see U.S., Congress, *Report of the Joint Committee on the Conduct of the War*, 38th Cong., 2d sess., "Red River Expedition," vol. 2, pp. 270–80. Hereafter cited as *Committee Report, Red River*.

29. Richard Taylor to Edmund Kirby-Smith, March 16, 1864, *Official Records*, vol. 34, pt. 1, pp. 463–64; Taylor, *Destruction and Reconstruction*, pp. 154–57.

30. Richard Taylor to Edmund Kirby-Smith, March 31, 1864, *Official Records*, vol. 34, pt. 1, pp. 510–17.

31. See Robert Underwood Johnson and Clarence Clough Buel, eds., *Battles and Leaders of the Civil War*, vol. 4, pp. 366–67. Therein are listed the forces under Banks's command.

32. *Committee Report, Red River*, pp. 281–84; David Porter to Nathaniel Banks, March 26, 1864, *Official Records, Navy*, vol. 26, pp. 50–52.

33. David Porter to Nathaniel Banks, March 26, 1864, *Official Records, Navy*, vol. 26, pp. 50–52.

34. *Committee Report, Red River*, pp. 283–86.

35. Ibid.

36. Richard B. Irwin, "The Red River Campaign," in Johnson and Buel, *Battles and Leaders*, vol. 4, p. 350.

37. *Committee Report, Red River*, pp. 35–41, 282–86.

38. Johnson and Buel, *Battles and Leaders*, p. 368; Irwin, "Red River Campaign," pp. 351–52; Taylor, *Destruction and Reconstruction*, pp. 157–58.

39. Richard Taylor to Edmund Kirby-Smith, March 31, 1864, *Official Records*, vol. 34, pt. 1, pp. 511–19.

40. Ibid.; Edmund Kirby-Smith to Richard Taylor, April 3, 1864, ibid., pp. 520–25.

41. Edmund Kirby-Smith to Richard Taylor, April 3, 1864, ibid.

42. See *Committee Report, Red River* (several eyewitness accounts of the events at Pleasant Hill are contained in the report); *Official Records*, vol. 34, pt. 1, pp. 286–91.

43. *Official Records*, vol. 34, pt. 1, pp. 286–91.

44. Ibid.; *Committee Report, Red River*, pp. 60–68; Irwin, "Red River Campaign," pp. 353–55.

45. Irwin, "Red River Campaign," p. 354.

46. Ibid., pp. 353–55; Richard Taylor to Edmund Kirby-Smith, April 10, 1864, *Official Records*, vol. 34, pt. 1, pp. 563–64; *Committee Report, Red River*, pp. 58–62; Dimitry, "Louisiana," pp. 142–43.

47. Dimitry, "Louisiana," vol. 14, pp. 142–43.

48. Ibid.; see Frank Moore, ed., *The Rebellion Record: A Diary of American Events*, vol. 8, pp. 545–49.

49. Moore, *Rebellion Record*, vol. 8, 545–49.

50. Ibid.

51. Ibid., p. 452; Taylor, *Destruction and Reconstruction*, p. 164.

52. Taylor, *Destruction and Reconstruction*, pp. 164–65; *Committee Report, Red River*, pp. 175–200; Confederate Reports, *Official Records*, ser. 1, vol. 34, pt. 1, pp. 563–67.

53. Ibid.

54. Ibid.

55. Irwin, "Red River Campaign," pp. 355–56; Edmund Kirby-Smith, "Defense of the Red River," in Johnson and Buel, *Battles and Leaders*, vol. 4, pp. 372–73.

56. Edmund Kirby-Smith, "Defense of the Red River," pp. 372–73.

57. Thomas O. Selfridge, "The Navy in the Red River," in Johnson and Buel, *Battles and Leaders*, vol. 4, pp. 362–63; *Committee Report, Red River*, pp. 275–76; Union Reports, *Official Records, Navy*, vol. 36, pp. 59–60; ibid., vol. 17, pp. 104–105; Bern Anderson, *By Sea and by River: The Naval History of the Civil War* (New York: Alfred A. Knopf, 1962), pp. 256–62; Fletcher Pratt, *Civil War on Western Waters* (New York: Henry Holt and Co., 1956), pp. 189–200; H. Allen Gosnell, *Guns on the Western Waters: The Story of River Gunboats in the Civil War* (Baton Rouge: Louisiana State University Press, 1949), pp. 246–66.

58. *Committee Report, Red River*, p. 203; Union Reports, *Official Records*, ser. 1, vol. 1, pt. 1, p. 452; Nathaniel Banks to David Porter, April 9, ibid., pt. 3, pp. 98–99.

59. *Committee Report, Red River*, pp. 8–9.

60. Ibid.

61. Ibid.

62. Selfridge, "Navy in the Red River," pp. 364–66; Kirby-Smith, "Defense of the Red River," pp. 372–73; Union Reports, *Official Records*, ser. 1, vol. 34, pt. 3, pp. 193–211.

63. Taylor, *Destruction and Reconstruction*, pp. 180–82; Richard Taylor to Edmund Kirby-Smith, April 18, 1864, *Official Records*, ser. 1, vol. 34, pt. 3, pp. 193–211.

64. Selfridge, "Navy in the Red River," p. 363.

65. Ibid., pp. 363–64; Kirby-Smith, "Defense of the Red River," p. 373; Odie B. Faulk, *A Fight'n Texan* (Waco: Texian Press, 1964), pp. 86–87.

66. Union Reports, *Official Records*, ser. 1, vol. 34, pt. 1, p. 382.

67. William T. Sherman to Nathaniel Banks, April 12, 1864, ibid., ser. 1, vol. 32, pt. 3, p. 24; Nathaniel Banks to U. S. Grant, April 13, 1864, ibid., ser. 1, vol. 34, pt. 3, pp. 187–88; Nathaniel Banks to William T. Sherman, April 14, 1864, ibid., ser. 1, pt. 3., vol. 34, pp. 265–66; David Porter to William T. Sherman, April 14, 1864, *Official Records, Navy*, vol. 26, p. 56; *Committee Report, Red River*, p. 278.

68. Union Reports, *Official Records, Navy*, vol. 26, pp. 62–69.

69. David Porter to William T. Sherman, April 14, 1864, ibid., vol. 26, p. 56.

70. Ibid., vol. 25, pp. 72–79; Selfridge, "Navy in the Red River," pp. 363–64.

71. Bragg, *Louisiana in the Confederacy*, p. 171; Johnson, *Red River Campaign*, pp. 224–26; Richard Taylor to S. S. Anderson, April 24, 1864, *Official Records*, ser. 1, vol. 34, pt. 1, pp. 580–81; Richard Taylor to S. S. Anderson, April 25, 1864, ibid., p. 581.

72. Richard Taylor to S. S. Anderson, April 25, 1864, *Official Records*, ser. 1, vol. 34, pt. 1, pp. 580–81; Taylor, *Destruction and Reconstruction*, p. 193.

73. Kirby-Smith, "Defense of the Red River," p. 373.

74. Taylor, *Destruction and Reconstruction*, p. 180; Richard Taylor to S. S. Anderson, April 24, 1864, *Official Records*, ser. 1, vol. 39, pt. 1, pp. 580–81.

75. Union Reports, *Official Records, Navy*, vol. 26, pp. 71–77.

76. Union Reports, *Official Records*, ser. 1, vol. 39, pt. 3, p. 317.

77. Union Reports, *Official Records, Navy*, vol. 31, pp. 131–35.

78. Ibid.; Selfridge, "Navy in the Red River," p. 358; Nathaniel Banks to David Porter, May 9, 1864, *Official Records, Navy*, vol. 26, p. 136; Nathaniel Banks to David Porter, May 9, 1864, ibid.

79. *Committee Reports, Red River*, p. 82.

80. Ibid.; Union Reports, *Official Records, Navy*, vol. 26, p. 131.

81. Ibid., p. 132; Kirby-Smith, "Defense of the Red River," p. 373.

82. Henry W. Halleck to U. S. Grant, April 30, 1864, *Official Records*, ser. 1, vol. 34, pt. 3, p. 357; Henry W. Halleck to Nathaniel Banks, April 30, 1864, ibid., p. 358.

CHAPTER 9

1. N. Philip Norman, "The Red River of the South," *Louisiana Historical Quarterly*, vol. 25, no. 2 (April, 1942), pp. 397–535.

2. Corps of Engineers, *Report of the Chief Engineer*, 1870, pp. 664–65.

3. Ibid., 1870, p. 648.

4. Ibid.

5. Ibid., 1873, pp. 64, 613–18.

6. Ibid., p. 615.

7. Ibid., p. 616.

8. Ibid., p. 618; ibid., 1905, pp. 1011–20.

9. Ibid., 1873, pp. 618, 628–30, 706–708; ibid., 1874, pp. 72, 703–705; ibid., 1875, pp. 523–29.

10. Ibid., 1875, p. 528; ibid., 1881, pp. 1405–1407.

11. Ibid., 1883, pp. 1138–40.

12. Ibid., pp. 1138–40.

13. Ibid., 1884, pp. 1321–30; ibid., 1885, pp. 1471–83.

14. Ibid., 1885, pp. 1471–83.

15. Ibid.

16. Ibid., 1890, pp. 1828–33.

17. Ibid., p. 1831.

18. Ibid., 1891, pp. 1963–69.

19. Ibid.

20. Ibid., 1895, pp. 1848–56.

21. Ibid.

22. Ibid., 1898, pp. 1575–91.

23. Ibid., 1900, pp. 2491–3002.

24. Ibid., 1909, p. 1319.

CHAPTER 10

1. U.S., Congress, House, Executive Document no. 635, 57th Cong., 1st sess., vol. 202, pp. 12–14.

2. D. Hunter Miller, *Treaties and Other International Acts of the United States of America*, vol. 3, p. 304; U.S., Congress, *Annals of Congress*, vol. 16, 1820, pp.

1501–1504. The text of the treaty is also printed in Philip C. Brooks, *Diplomacy and the Borderlands*, pp. 205–14.

3. John Sayles and Henry Sayles, eds., *Early Laws of Texas*, vol. 1, pp. 568–69.

4. Governor Sam Houston to William H. Russell, April 30, 1860, Executive Record Book, Houston, 1859–61.

5. U.S., Congress, Senate, Document no. 70, 47th Cong., 1st sess., vol. 3.

6. Sayles, *Laws of Texas*, vol. 2, pp. 2886–87; U.S., Congress, House, Document no. 1595, 2d sess., vol. 5; H. P. N. Gammel, *Laws of Texas*, vol. 9, pp. 127–28.

7. U.S., Congress, House, *Journal of the House*, 47th Cong., 1st sess., p. 20; U.S., Congress, House, Document no. 1282, 47th Cong., 1st sess., vol. 5; U.S., Congress, Senate, Document no. 314, 47th Cong., 1st sess., vol. 1.

8. See "The United States Complainent Versus the State of Texas in Equity," *Record of the Supreme Court of the United States, October Term, 1891*, vol. 1, p. 25; Grant Foreman, "The Red River and the Spanish Boundary," *Chronicles of Oklahoma*, vol. 2, no. 3 (January, 1925), pp. 38–47.

9. U.S., Congress, House, Document no. 99, 48th Cong., 2d sess., vol. 5.

10. U.S., Congress, House, Executive Document no. 21, 50th Cong., 1st sess., vol. 18, p. 5.

11. Ibid.

12. Ibid., p. 9.

13. Ibid.

14. Ibid.

15. Ibid.

16. Ibid.

17. Ibid.

18. Ibid.

19. Ibid., p. 10.

20. Ibid.

21. Ibid., pp. 9–23.

22. Ibid., p. 163.

23. Ibid., p. 164.

24. U.S., Congress, House, Executive Document no. 404, 51st Cong., 1st sess., vol. 37.

25. "The United States Complainent Versus the State of Texas in Equity," *United States Reports*, vol. 162, p. 102; vol. 143, pp. 143, 625.

26. Ibid., pp. 630–48.

27. Ibid., pp. 20–90.

28. Ibid., p. 90.

29. See Claude A. Welborn, *The Red River Controversy* (Wichita Falls, Texas: Nortex Co., 1973); Webb L. Moore, *The Greer County Question* (n.p., 1939).

30. U.S., Congress, House, Document no. 38, 59th Cong., 1st sess.

31. Ibid.

32. Dale McKinney, "A Century of Dissension at the Red River Boundary" (master's thesis, Oklahoma State University, 1941), pp. 34–47; James A. Barnett, "The Empire of Greer" (master's thesis, Oklahoma State University, 1938), pp. 55–61; *U.S. L.Ed.*, vol. 39, pp. 876–99.

33. McKinney, "Red River Boundary," pp. 51–52.

34. 258 *U.S. L.Ed.*, vol. 64, p. 779; Isaiah Bowman, "An American Boundary Dispute," *Geographical Review*, vol. 13 (1923), pp. 163–65.

35. Bowman, "American Boundary," pp. 163–65; *Original Supreme Court Transcript*, vol. 20, pp. 2644–49.

36. Earnest Knaebel, Reporter, *Cases Adjusted in the Supreme Court*, vol. 258, p. 582; McKinney, "Red River Boundary," p. 62.

37. *United States Reports*, vol. 252, p. 372; "The State of Oklahoma Complainant versus the State of Texas, Defendant, United States of America Intervenor," *Record of the Supreme Court of the United States, October Term, 1920, no. 23 Original*, p. 85.

38. "The State of Oklahoma Complainant versus the State of Texas, Defendant, United States of America Intervenor," *Record of the Supreme Court of the United States, October Term, 1920, no. 23 Original*, p. 90.

39. Ibid., p. 92.

40. *U.S. Reports*, vol. 258, p. 280.

41. "Oklahoma versus Texas, United States, Intervenor," *U.S. Reports*, vol. 256, p. 70; 258 *U.S. L.Ed.*, vol. 65, p. 772; Knaebel, *Cases Adjusted in the Supreme Court October Term 1922*, vol. 258, p. 582.

42. McKinney, "Red River Boundary," pp. 66–71; Leonidas Glenn, "Geology and Physiography of the Red River Boundary Between Texas and Oklahoma," *Pan American Geologist*, vol. 43, no. 2 (Spring, 1925), pp. 365–68; E. H. Sellards, "The Oklahoma-Texas Boundary Suit," *Science*, vol. 62, no. 1 (March, 1923), pp. 340–52.

43. 258 *U.S. L.Ed.*, vol. 65, p. 772.

44. Ibid., pp. 770–72; McKinney, "Red River Boundary," pp. 63–68.

45. McKinney, "Red River Boundary," pp. 63–68; 258 *U.S. L.Ed.*, vol. 65, p. 772.

46. McKinney, "Red River Boundary," pp. 71–72; Sellards, "Oklahoma-Texas Boundary Suit," p. 347.

47. Sellards, "Oklahoma-Texas Boundary Suit," p. 347.

48. Ibid.

49. *U.S. Reports*, vol. 258, p. 574; ibid., vol. 261, pp. 340–50.

50. Sellards, "Oklahoma-Texas Boundary Suit," p. 348.

CHAPTER 11

1. U.S., Congress, House, Document no. 308, 69th Cong., 1st sess.; Document no. 378, 74th Cong., 2d sess.

2. U.S., Congress, House, no. 378, pp. 249–50.

3. Ibid., p. 129.

4. Ibid.

5. Ibid., pp. 385, 393–94.

6. Ibid., pp. 129–30.

7. Ibid., p. 130.

8. Ibid.

9. *Arkansas and Red River Basins* (Corps of Engineers pamphlet), pp. 39–45.

10. *Pub.L.* no. 409, 74th Cong.; *Pub.L.* no. 293, 75th Cong.; *Pub.L.* no. 685, 75th Cong.
11. U.S., Congress, House, Document no. 320, 80th Cong., 1st sess., p. 2. See also ibid., pp. 17–18.
12. Ibid., pp. 17–18; see also ibid., p. 10.
13. Ibid.; *Pub.L.* no. 534, 78th Cong.; *Pub.L.* no. 526, 79th Cong.
14. *Pub.L.* no. 516, 81st Cong.
15. U.S., Congress, Senate, Document no. 13, 85th Cong., 1st sess.
16. Ibid., pp. 954–55.
17. *Pub.L.* no. 160, 84th Cong.; *Pub.L.* no. 500, 85th Cong.; U.S., Congress, House, Document no. 170, 85th Cong., 2d sess.; U.S., Congress, Senate, Document no. 132, 87th Cong., 2d sess.; U.S., Congress, Senate, Document no. 144, 87th Cong., 2d sess.; U.S., Congress, Senate, Document no. 145, 87th Cong., 2d sess.
18. *Pub.L.* no. 500, 85th Cong.
19. *Pub.L.* no. 874, 87th Cong.
20. *Arkansas and Red River Basins*, pp. 39–45.
21. Ibid., p. 39.
22. U.S., Congress, Senate, Document no. 13, 85th Cong., 1st sess., p. 791; *Arkansas and Red River Basins*, p. 39.

Selected Bibliography

I. PRIMARY SOURCES

Bexar Archives, University of Texas Archives, Austin.

Dunbar, William. *Life, Letters, and Papers of William Dunbar.* Ed. Eron Rowland. Jackson, Miss.: Press of Mississippi Historical Society, 1930.

Freeman, Thomas, and Custis, Peter. *An Account of the Red River in Louisiana Drawn Up from the Returns of Messrs. Freeman and Custis to the War Office of the United States, Who Explored the Same in the Year 1806.* Washington, D.C., n.p., 1807.

Gammel, H. P. N. *Laws of Texas.* 10 vols. Austin, Texas: Gammel Book Co., 1930.

Jefferson, Thomas. *The Writings of Thomas Jefferson.* Ed. Paul L. Ford. 26 vols. New York: G. P. Putnam's Sons, 1897.

Letterbook of the Natchitoches Indian Factory, Office of Indian Affairs, National Archives.

Margry, Pierre, ed. *Decouvertes et etablissements des français dans l'ouest et dans le sud de l'Amérique Septentrionale.* 6 vols. Paris: Imprimerie de D. Jouaust et Sigaux, 1879–1888.

Nathan, Paul, ed. and trans. *The San Sabá Papers.* San Francisco: J. Howell, 1959.

New Mexico Archives, State of New Mexico Records Center, Santa Fe, New Mexico.

Pike, Zebulon Montgomery. *The Expedition of Zebulon Montgomery Pike to Headwaters of the Mississippi River, Through Louisiana Territory, and in New Spain, During the Years 1805–6–7.* Ed. Elliott Coves. 3 vols. New York: Francis Harper, 1895.

Sayles, John, and Sayles, Henry, eds. *Early Laws of Texas.* 2 vols. St. Louis: Gilbert Book Co., 1891.

Wallace, Ernest, and Vigness, David M., eds. *Documents of Texas History*. Austin: Steck Co., 1963.

II. FEDERAL AND STATE GOVERNMENT DOCUMENTS

Annals of Congress, U.S. Congress. 9th Congress. 1st sess. 1805–1806.

————, U.S. Congress, 15th Congress, 2nd sess. 1819.

————, U.S. Congress, 16th Congress, 2nd sess. 1819–1820.

Arkansas and Red River Basins, Corps of Engineers Pamphlet, Tulsa District.

Census for 1820 (Fourth Census). Washington, D.C.: Gales and Seaton, 1821. Bk. 1.

Executive Record Book. Houston, 1857–61. Archives, Texas State Library, Austin.

Knaebel, Ernest. *Cases Adjusted in the Supreme Court*. 50 vols. Washington, D.C.: Government Printing Office, 1922–35.

Letter from Dr. Joseph Paxton, of Hempstead County, to the Hon. A. H. Sevier Delegate to Congress from the Territory of Arkansas, in Relation to the Raft of Red River. U.S., Congress, House. Document no. 78. 20th Cong., 2d sess.

Marcy, Randolph B. *Explorations of the Red River of Louisiana in the year 1852*. U.S., Congress, Senate. Executive Document no. 54. 32d Cong., 2d sess.

Miller, D. Hunter. *Treaties and Other International Acts of the United States of America*. 5 vols. Washington, D.C.: Government Printing Office, 1820.

Official Record of the Union and Confederate Navies in the War of the Rebellion. 30 vols. Washington, D.C.: Government Printing Office, 1905.

Record of the Supreme Court of the United States. Congress, House. Document no. 378. 74th Cong., 2d. sess.

Red River, La., Ark., Okla., and Texas. U.S., Congress, House. Document no. 378. 74th Cong., 2d. sess.

Report of the Chief Engineer of the Army. Washington, D.C.: Government Printing Office, 1870–1909.

The Seventh Census of the United States: 1850. Washington, D.C.: Robert Armstrong, 1853.

U.S., Congress, House. Document no. 78. 20th Cong., 2d sess.

————, House. Document no. 98. 23d Cong., 1st sess.

————, House. Document no. 1. 25th Cong., 1st sess.

————, House. Document no. 24. 33d Cong., 1st sess.

————, House. Document no. 1282. vol. 10. 47th Cong., 1st sess.

————, House. Document no. 99. vol. 5. 48th Cong., 2d sess.

————, House. *State Papers and Correspondence Bearing upon the Purchase of the Territory of Louisiana.* Document no. 431. 5 vols. 57th Cong., 2d sess.

————, House. Document no. 38. 59th Cong., 1st sess.

————, House. Document no. 308. 69th Cong., 1st sess.

————, House. Document no. 320. 80th Cong., 1st sess.

————, House. Document no. 170. 85th Cong., 1st sess.

————, House. Executive Document no. 404, vol. 37. 51st Cong., 1st sess.

————, House. *Journal of the House.* 47th Cong., 1st sess.

————, *Report of the Joint Committee on the Conduct of the War.* 38th Cong., 2d sess. vol. 2.

————, Senate. Document no. 64. 27th Cong., 1st sess.

————, Senate. Document no. 314. 47th Cong., 1st sess. vol. 1.

————, Senate. *Development of Water and Land Resources of the Arkansas-White and Red River Basins.* Document no. 13. 85th Cong., 1st sess.

————, Senate. Document no. 105. 87th Cong., 2d sess.

————, Senate. Document no. 145. 87th Cong., 2d sess.

War of the Rebellion, The: A Compilation of the Official Records of the Union and Confederate Armies. 70 vols., 128 bks. Washington, D.C.: Government Printing Office, 1880–1901.

III. BOOKS

Anderson, Melville B., ed. *Joutel's Journal of La Salle's Last Voyage.* New York: Burt Franklin, 1968.

Bemis, Samuel Flagg. *John Quincy Adams and the Foundation of American Foreign Policy.* New York: Alfred A. Knopf, 1950.

Bolton, Herbert Eugene, ed. *Athanase de Mézières and the Louisiana-Texas Frontier, 1768–1780.* 2 vols. Cleveland: Arthur H. Clark Co., 1914.

————. *Texas in the Middle of the Eighteenth Century.* Berkeley: University of California Press, 1915.

Bonnell, George. *Topographical Description of Texas*. 1840. Reprint. Waco: Texian Press, 1964.

Bragg, Jefferson Davis. *Louisiana in the Confederacy*. Baton Rouge: Louisiana State University Press, 1941.

Brooks, Philip C. *Diplomacy and the Borderlands: The Adams-Onís Treaty of 1819*. Berkeley: University of California Press, 1939.

Castañeda, Carlos E. *Our Catholic Heritage in Texas*. 7 vols. Austin: Von Boeckmann-Jones Co., 1931–58.

Cox, Isaac J. "The Exploration of the Louisiana Frontier, 1803–1806." *Annual Report of the American Historical Association for 1904*. Washington, D.C.: Government Printing Office, 1905.

Dangerfield, George. *The Awakening of American Nationalism*. New York: Harper and Row, 1952.

Dunn, William E. *Spanish and French Rivalry in the Gulf Region of the United States, 1678–1702*. Studies in History, no. 1. University of Texas Bulletin no. 1705, January 20, 1917.

Faulk, Odie B. *The Last Years of Spanish Texas*. The Hague: Mouton and Co., 1964.

——. *A Successful Failure*. Austin: Steck-Vaughn Co., 1965.

Garretson, Martin S. *The American Bison*. New York: New York Zoological Society, 1938.

Gayarre, Charles. *Louisiana: Its Colonial History and Romance*. New York: Harper and Brothers, 1851.

Hakluyt, Richard, trans. *The Discovery and Conquest of Terra Florida by Don Ferdinando de Soto and Six Hundred Spaniards His Followers* (1611). Edited by William B. Rye. New York: Burt Franklin, 1963.

Hammond, George P., and Rey, Agapito, eds. *Narratives of the Coronado Expedition, 1540–1542*, 2 vols. Albuquerque: University of New Mexico Press, 1940.

Hatcher, Mattie Austin. *The Opening of Texas to Foreign Settlement*. University of Texas Bulletin no. 2714, 1927.

Hodge, Frederick W., ed. *Handbook of American Indians North of Mexico*, 2 vols. New York: Pageant Books, 1959.

Hyde, H. Montgomery. *John Law: The History of an Honest Adventurer*. Denver: Alan Swallow, 1948.

Indian Tribes of Texas. Waco: Texian Press, 1971.

Johnson, Ludwell H. *Red River Campaign: Politics and Cotton in the Civil War*. Baltimore: Johns Hopkins Press, 1958.

Johnson, Robert Underwood, and Buel, Clarence Clough, eds. *Battles and Leaders of the Civil War*. 4 vols. New York: Thomas Yoseloff, 1956.

Lewis, Anna. *Along the Arkansas*. Dallas: Southwest Press, 1932.

Loomis, Noel M., and Nasatir, Abraham P. *Pedro Vial and the Roads to Santa Fe*. Norman: University of Oklahoma Press, 1967.

Lynch, John. *The Spanish American Revolution, 1808–1826*. New York: W. W. Norton and Co., 1973.

McCaleb, Walter Flavius. *The Aaron Burr Conspiracy*. New York: Wilson-Erickson, 1936.

Moore, Frank, ed. *The Rebellion Record: A Diary of American Events*. vols. New York, 1862–71.

Morfi, Juan A. *History of Texas, 1673–1779*. Ed. and trans. Carlos E. Casteñeda. Albuquerque: Quivira Society, 1935.

Murphy, Edmund R. *Henry de Tonty: Fur Trader of the Mississippi*. Baltimore: Johns Hopkins Press, 1941.

Nathan, Paul, ed., and trans. *The San Sabá Papers*. San Francisco: J. Howell, 1959.

Parkman, Francis. *La Salle and the Discovery of the Great West*. Boston: Little, Brown and Co., 1927.

Phares, Ross. *Cavalier of the Wilderness*. Baton Rouge: Louisiana State University Press, 1952.

Reed, Charles B. *The First Great Canadian: The Story of Pierre le Moyne, Sieur D'Iberville*. Chicago: A. C. McClurg and Co., 1910.

Sherman, William T. *Memoirs of Gen. W. T. Sherman*. 2 vols. New York: Charles L. Webster and Co., 1892.

Taylor, Richard. *Destruction and Reconstruction: Personal Experiences of the Late War*. New York: D. Appleton and Co., 1890.

Thomas, Alfred Barnaby. *Teodoro de Croix and the Northern Frontier of New Spain, 1776–1783*. Norman: University of Oklahoma Press, 1941.

Wallace, Ernest, and Hoebel, E. Adamson. *The Comanches: Lords of the South Plains*. University of Oklahoma Press, 1952.

Webb, Walter P., ed. *The Handbook of Texas*. 2 vols. Austin: Texas State Historical Society, 1952.

Weddle, Robert W. *The San Sabá Mission: Spanish Pivot in Texas*. Austin: University of Texas Press, 1964.

———. *Wilderness Manhunt: The Spanish Search for La Salle*. Austin: University of Texas Press, 1972.

211

Wheat, Andrew. *Mapping the American West: A Preliminary Study.* Worcester, Mass.: American Antiquarian Society, 1954.

IV. ARTICLES

Barr, Alwyn. "Texas Coastal Defenses, 1861–1865." *Southwestern Historical Quarterly* vol. 65, no. 11 (July, 1965), pp. 1–31.

Bolton, Herbert Eugene. "Native Tribes About the East Texas Missions." *Quarterly of the Texas State Historical Association* vol. 11, no. 4 (April, 1908), pp. 249–276.

Bowman, Isaiah. "An American Boundary Dispute." *Geographic Review* vol. 13, (1923), pp. 163–175.

Bugbee, Lester G. "The Real Saint-Denis." *Quarterly of the Texas State Historical Association* vol. 1, no. 4 (April, 1898), pp. 216–281.

Clark, Robert C. "The Beginnings of Texas." *Quarterly of the Texas State Historical Association* vol. 10, no. 3 (January, 1902), pp. 171–205.

————. "Louis Juchereau de Saint-Denis and the Re-Establishment of the Tejas Missions." *Quarterly of the Texas State Historical Association* vol. 6, no. 1 (July, 1902), pp. 1–26.

Coopwood, Bethel. "Notes on the History of La Bahía Del Espíritu Santo." *Quarterly of the Texas State Historical Association* vol. 2, no. 2 (October, 1898), pp. 162–169.

Cox, Isaac J. "The Louisiana-Texas Frontier." *Quarterly of the Texas State Historical Association* vol. 10, no. 1 (Summer, 1906), pp. 1–75.

————. "The Texas-Louisiana Frontier." *Quarterly of the Texas State Historical Association* vol. 10, no. 2 (Summer, 1908), pp. 30–45.

Dunn, Milton. "History of Natchitoches." *Louisiana Historical Quarterly* vol. 3, no. 1 (January, 1920), pp. 26–56.

Estill-Harbour, Emma. "A Brief History of the Red River Country Since 1803." *Chronicles of Oklahoma* vol. 16, no. 1 (March, 1938), pp. 58–67.

Faulk, Odie B. "The Comanche Invasion of Texas, 1743–1836." *Great Plains Journal* vol. 9, no. 1 (Fall, 1969), pp. 1–51.

Glenn, Leonidas. "Geology and Physiography of the Red River Boundary Between Texas and Oklahoma." *Pan American Geologist* vol. 43, no. 2 (Spring, 1925), pp. 360–371.

Hill, Robert T. "The Topography and Geology of the Cross Timbers and Surrounding Regions in Northern Texas." *American Journal of Science*, 3d ser., vol. 33 (1887), pp. 34–49.

Manzanet, Damián. "Carta de Don Carlos de Siquienza sobre el descubrimento de la Bahía del Espíritu Santo." *Quarterly of the Texas State Historical Association* vol. 2, no. 4 (April, 1899), pp. 254–280. English translation by Lilia A. Casis, pp. 281–312.

Norman, Philip N. "The Red River of the South." *Louisiana Historical Quarterly* vol. 25, no. 2 (April, 1952), pp. 397–535.

Satcher, Buford. "Louisiana: Six Hundred Engagements." *Journal of the West* vol. 14, no. 1 (January, 1975), pp. 149–166.

Schmitt, E. J. P. "Who was Juchereau de Saint-Denis?" *Quarterly of the Texas State Historical Society* vol. 1, no. 3 (January, 1898), pp. 204–215.

Shelby, Charmoin C. "St. Denis's Declaration Concerning Texas in 1717." *Southwestern Historical Quarterly* vol. 26, no. 3 (January, 1923), pp. 165–171.

———. "St. Denis's Second Expedition to the Río Grande, 1716–1719." *Southwestern Historical Quarterly* vol. 27, no. 3 (January, 1924), pp. 190–216.

Tyson, Carl Newton. "Texas: Men for War; Cotton for Economy." *Journal of the West* vol. 14, no. 1 (January, 1975), pp. 130–48.

West, Elizabeth H. "De Leon's Expedition of 1689." *Quarterly of the Texas State Historical Association* vol. 8, no. 3 (January, 1905), pp. 199–224.

Wright, Muriel. "Early Navigation and Commerce Along the Arkansas and Red Rivers in Oklahoma." *Chronicles of Oklahoma* vol. 8, no. 1 (March, 1927), pp. 65–88.

V. MASTER'S THESES

Barnett, James A. "The Empire of Greer." Oklahoma A&M College [Oklahoma State University], 1938.

Cox, Charles Raymond. "Caddoan Relations with the White Race Previous to 1801." Oklahoma A&M College, 1930.

McKinney, Dale. "A Century of Dissension at the Red River Boundary." Oklahoma A&M College, 1941.

Index

215